Promises to Keep:
Crafting Your Wedding Ceremony

Rites to Remember Series

Promises to Keep:
Crafting Your Wedding Ceremony

Remembering a Life:
On the Death of Your Beloved

Rites to Remember

Promises to Keep:

Crafting Your Wedding Ceremony

Ann Keeler Evans, M.Div.

Emerald Earth Publishing

Promises to Keep:
Crafting Your Wedding Ceremony

Copyright © 2001 Ann Keeler Evans
Published by Emerald Earth Publishing
PO Box 1946, Sebastopol, California 95473
707/829-0868   www.EmeraldEarth.net

Book Design: Julie Middleton
Art: Sylvia Sims

Evans, Ann Keeler, author, 1952-
    Promises to Keep: Crafting Your Wedding Ceremony / Ann Keeler Evans
Sebastopol, CA: Emerald Earth Publishing, 2001
    p. 120   cm.

    ISBN 0-9663715-3-4
    1. Weddings 2. Rites and Ceremonies I. Title
395.22 dc21

To those who clapped for Tinkerbell
and who kept her in fairy dust —
and to my clients, who dare to believe in forever.

I never understood the importance of acknowledgments until
I went to seminary. And then I got listed in someone's acknowledgment
and it felt great to be recognized for contributing to their lives.
So here I am, at long last able to turn to my friends and family
and say a public "thank you."
Thank you not only for your contributions
to my thinking and my ceremony-making,
but thank you for the ways in which we share our lives,
for the food and laughter and tears and tai chi and babies and music
and lazy Sunday afternoons.
You make my life holy by your existence.

Thanks to: Amy, Barry, Clint, Deb, Doug, Ed, Ellen, Ellie, Hillair,
Jennifer June, Jess, JoAnne, Kim, Linda, Maggie, Rob and Scout for your
unwavering support; to The Church Ladies, who taught me how hard and
how much fun it is to be a priestess; Remy and Sara; Karen; Peg and
Alexandra; Maggie, Steve and Hannah; Michael; Connie; Pierre; Carolyn
and Jim; Amanda and Rebecca and Zane; Pete, Susan and Dustin, Monte,
Katie and Max; Doug and Linnea; Eda, Stephen and Stella; The Barbs,
Chuck, Miguel, David and Chris, Johanna and Suzanne, Cara, Tyson,
Camper and Boojum for being my friends and my support. Lizzie, Rodger,
Erik, Lorraine and Dorothy and all their family for my place in their lives.
Kara and Dave, Nina and the whole family gang, who supported me,
believed in me and offered me so many great opportunities to do my work.

And last, but hardly least, Sam and Betty, Roberta, Tom, Cindy, Wayne,
Nancy, Doug, Ellen, Wayne, Kate, Jan, Karen, Lindsay, Jeremy, Jen, Earie,
Chad, Elijah, Sarrah, Tom, and Julia:
my family, who love me and believe in me.
My dears, we have indeed celebrated together!

Contents

Foreword   9

Introduction   11

1 – So, What Is Marriage, Anyway?   13
     What Is Marriage Now?   14
     Why Are You Doing This?   16
     How Do You Want to Shape Your Marriage?   17
     What Is Faithfulness?   18
     What Is the Long View?   20

2 – Why Not Elope?   22
     What Ritual Does   24
     What Ritual Isn't   24
     Public Ritual Changes Lives   25
     A Safe Environment for You   25
     Ritual and Community   27
     What Is Meaning? Why Does It Matter?   29
     You Are a Part of This Community   29
     Design Adaptable Ritual   30
     The Place   30
     Rehearsal   31

3 – Crafting Your Ceremony   33
     Introduction / Invitation   34
     Invocation   36
         Ritual Space   36
         The Unbroken Circle   38
         What Do You Believe?   38
     Joining Your Families   41
     Statement of Intent   43
     Statement of Support   45
     Images of Relationship   48
     Charge to the Couple   51
     Vows   52
     Exchange of Rings   54
     Proclamation   55
     Blessing   56

Benediction 59
4—Rituals from the Heart 61
Ceremonies of Faith and Family 61
Chuppa 62
Chinese Tea Ceremony 63
Origami Peace Cranes 64
Unity Candle 65
Breaking the Glass 67
Binding the Couple Together 69
Flower Ceremonies 69
Dedication Ceremonies 73

5 – When You Don't Fit the Mold 75
Second Marriages 75
Relinquishing Past Promises 75
Wonderful Memories 77
Children from Former Relationships 78
Commitment Ceremonies for Lesbians and Gay Men ... 81
Handfasting 83
Renewal of Vows 85

6 – Your Family Is Always Your Family 87
Disapproving Parents 87
Unfriendly Family Breakups 89
Notes for Parents 90
Parents Unhappy with Your Sexual Orientation ... 91
Parents Unhappy You Are Marrying Outside Your Clan ... 93
Family Dynamics and Issues 94

7 – Where to Find Your Celebrant 96
Do You Want a Religious or Secular Ceremony? ... 97
Your States' Laws About Celebrants 97
Great Weddings You've Been To 98
Services Vary 98
Interview the Candidates 99
Fees: Expect to Pay for What You Want 99

8 – Benediction 101

Appendix 103

Foreword

At last, from an accomplished theologian, an intelligent and imaginative alternative to the Martha Stewart school of wedding planning. *Promises to Keep* is a stunning and often appropriately humorous guide which elevates joining lives and making enduring promises above menus, centerpieces and place settings.

Promises to Keep is useful in every practical way for a wedding ceremony of meaning and depth. It goes beyond the couple and places the context of the ceremony in family and community; it addresses the practical, personal and spiritual needs of parents and friends.

Promises to Keep is broadly religious for a contemporary world where no one religion describes the whole of personal relationships; it is inclusive of many religious approaches and supports a unity of world religious traditions. It offers spiritual advice in an accessible, yet profound language that fits a variety of personal and family contexts.

Promises to Keep covers territory lost and forgotten in the landscape of rote and trivialized ritual so evident in our religious climate.

It thoughtfully plumbs ground like "love" and "transformation," and the couple's vows and what they mean; what's at the heart of the decision to marry; ceremony as a gift to self and community. And what is more, it gives samples of vows, lessons from the ceremonies of others — some which worked, some which did not. The Appendix provides worksheets to help couples think about the important spiritual and personal questions in concrete and simple ways.

I loved this book. I wish I had encountered Ann Keeler Evans' vision and imagination years ago when I first began to officiate at weddings. It would have enlarged my thinking and I'm sure it would have entranced the couples who came to me to share this uniquely important moment in their lives.

In an age hungry for meaning and hope, *Promises to Keep* serves it up like a spiritual Thanksgiving feast. This book will inspire anyone searching for integrity in their lifelong vows and commitments. This book is more than a practical wedding guide or spiritual handbook for beginning new lives: it's a blessing of wonderful proportion.

— The Rev. Barry L. Stopfel, Episcopal Priest
Executive Director of River Ministries

Introduction

Congratulations! You're engaged! All you need to do now is buy the wedding books, read the expensive magazines, sit down with the yellow pages — and you'll have all you need to plan your wedding, right? Well . . . almost.

Planning the wedding *ceremony* usually rates only a short section in wedding planners, if it's mentioned at all. And let's face it — while you've no doubt had great hors d'oeuvres at receptions, have you ever been to a truly memorable wedding ceremony? *The vows you will make to each other are at the heart of your wedding ceremony.*

Ritual and ceremony celebrate the way people live. Your wedding ritual and the promises you make become the trellis on which you plant the vine of your relationship — something to support you when times are troubled.

The purpose of this book is to help you design a personalized, meaningful ceremony which exactly suits the two of you and your relationship. When you stand before your community hand in hand, the commitments you're making to each other will allow your love to flourish for the rest of your lives.

Come! Let us celebrate together!

Chapter 1
So, What Is Marriage, Anyway?

The wedding ceremony originated as a financial transaction. The principal questions asked were "Who gives this bride?" (meaning, "Who owns this property?") and "Is there anyone here who knows of any reason why these two may not be joined?" (meaning, "Are there any outstanding liens on this property?"). The vows were the couple's agreement to abide by the family arrangements for the transfer of property.

Marriage was designed for the propagation of the species, the succession of property and power, and to maintain bloodlines and provide enough workers for the tasks of the family.

Family size and make up have always reflected the economy. In an agricultural society, many children were needed to work the farm. Nomadic men had many wives who produced many children that enabled them to graze as many herds as the tundra would accommodate. Up to this point, people lived tribally or in villages and depended upon each other to help out with special abilities. Someone could shear sheep, someone could doctor wounds, someone could midwife.

Then industrialization arrived. Tribes disappeared and families became smaller as they moved into the cities, and three generations were needed to provide care for the young and for the elders. Language abilities were often the common denominator, and you lived in ghettos of people you could talk to. Nuclear families really exploded as companies opened more branches and needed employees to move from place to place. Don't be fooled when you hear traditionalists talking about the old-time nuclear family: it's a fairly recent phenomenon.

What Is Marriage Now?

Today's society and economic structure do not support marriage, however facile the national discourse on the value of families. Few jobs pay enough for families to exist on one salary, so very often both adults are working. Work has replaced church, village and family life as the focus of most lives. It would be more convenient for employers if everyone were single and had no outside responsibilities — and think how high the consumer index would go if we all bought our own cars, houses, refrigerators! Tax rates are better for singles.

And there are very strict requirements about what constitutes a family — both legal and societal.

Marriage today is much more about equal partnership than it has ever been. "Traditional" marriage can now mean a wide spectrum of things. Even when one partner is the homemaker and child-rearer, this role is different than it was in an earlier time. I love to see the "Traditional Values Men" talking about marriage roles and having those discussions with a baby in their arms and a diaper bag on their shoulders. Good for them! Why shouldn't they share in the sweetness and sorrow of tending for children?

Shared activities at home are much more the norm. For example, Dad may be the partner staying at home, or Mom and Dad (or Dad and Dad) may take turns staying home. The home partner's role is a viable and important one, not ancillary or supportive of the wage earner's role. Many Gen Xers who marry today have paid a very high price for absent parents and are making the choice to have one partner at home with the kids — a tough financial decision. What tradition and society ask of a couple is different from what they say they want for a couple. As I've said in many ceremonies:

> As couples pledge their lives to one another at this point in history, they take on the challenges of living together in love. In addition they claim the responsibilities of reshaping and remaking an institution through which society has tried to define who was permitted to live together and what roles each person should play in that joining. These two are choosing to become each other's life partner. Hard work indeed!

So you're choosing to spend your lives together. Obviously, you don't need to get married to do that. You get married because you want to stand before your circle of friends and family to declare your love and seek their support.

Why Are You Doing This?

Your wedding is a time to be truthful with yourself. It's a wonderful opportunity to wrestle with what you believe about the institution of marriage, and your ability and willingness to participate in and transform it. In this process you can search for clarity about your intentions toward your beloved, and let others know how this person enriches your life. As you marry, you are asked to find and reveal your deepest truths and your sense of integrity.

Clearly articulated goals increase the chance a couple has of attaining a life-long relationship.

Fuzzy language celebrating hearts and flowers does not speak to the very hard work or the sweet laughter of shared lives. Accurate "snapshots" of the relationship and the desired long-term results help the couple answer the hardest question of relationship: why am I here? Clear goals help answer those questions now — when couples should struggle to find real answers to this question — and they help answer them as they arise in the future.

Few couples are asked why they have chosen to marry. When they are asked, often no one presses them beyond trite and romantic answers to this most important question. Being fathoms deep in love is helpful, but not reliable or enduring as the sole reason for marrying.

A little more thought might reveal a more powerful motivation: "This person calls me ever more deeply into myself and encourages me to take risks that enrich my life" — a wonderful reason to marry and one rarely heard mentioned at a wedding ceremony. "I wish to spend the rest of my life building a life and a family with this person" is a sentiment that needs to be clearly articulated, one that makes sense as the basis for life-long promises.

How Do You Want to Shape Your Marriage?

What is very important is to understand which qualities and activities you would like to have in your marriage, and which you would not.

Melissa and John wished to model their marriage on the interesting and successful partnerships they had seen between their parents and other adults, the acceptance and growth as partners. There were qualities in those marriages they definitely wanted to include, but they had also witnessed ways of interacting that they felt would be detrimental to their partnership. They were looking for a way to formalize their thoughts about these, but they didn't want to do it at the wedding, which should focus on their growing life together. They didn't wish to risk hurting someone's feelings by rejecting what might be a workable relationship for others simply because it would be unproductive in their lives.

I really enjoyed this couple and they were very willing to experiment with me, so I asked them each to prepare two lists. The first list detailed qualities or activities they absolutely wished to exclude from their marriage. Some of those were silly little reflex items that they had seen their parents or other married couples do, and that they wanted consciously to eliminate from their own patterns. Other qualities were simply inappropriate to the way they were choosing to live their lives: either representing an earlier model of men and women living in a marital relationship or qualities that they felt did not apply to who they were as individuals.

The second list enumerated qualities that they wished to call into their marriage. These might be things they saw in their parents' or friends' marriages, or something they hadn't seen but felt would enhance their partnership. Once the lists were completed, each read their negative list aloud and burned it, letting go of those qualities and banishing them from their marriage. Then they read their list of positive qualities and, casting it into the fire, called those qualities into their partnership. This burning ritual is based on two traditional ideas: one, that fire transforms paper and thought into action; and two, that smoke carries our words to the heavens. This is based on a Native American ritual I was taught and given permission to use, and the old saying in many languages: "From your mouth to God's ears."

You might also bury the lists, plant them, tear them up, toss them in a lake or the ocean. It can be helpful to simply write the lists and read them out loud, or post them where you will see them frequently. This process offers clarity about what is valued and what is seen as deterrent. What's important is to concentrate on those qualities you think would give life to your marriage and eliminate those you think might reduce your chances for a happy marriage.

What Is Faithfulness?

Faithfulness is often defined by people as being true to the literal meaning of the word. "If I don't touch someone or engage with them, I am not being unfaithful." But I think there is something much deeper to be explored. If promises are made to be present and available to your beloved, physical encounters are not the only hallmarks of being outside

18

relationship. Investing in daydreams about new relationships, when the tension in this one is unbearable, is equally unfaithful. *Faithfulness means being true to yourself and the promises you made, as well as being true to the one to whom you made these promises.* This has always been important; but today, with so much uncertainty about what marriage is and what roles we play inside it, our best tool is to be clear about our own integrity. This helps us to stay put and engaged in the process long enough to do the work to get to the other side of the struggle. I have hope for this rising generation of young marrieds because they have been such good friends during their courtship, and because they have been freed of many of the gender separations with which other generations have struggled.

And what about sex? Passion like everything else will ebb and flow in relationship, but between a committed couple passion can find its fullest expression — and it can be the riskiest. We risk opening ourselves and exposing our vulnerabilities with partners who truly know and love us. *I wonder if all the sexual problems we're hearing about don't have more to do with problems of being intimate when we're in periods of uncertainty in our lives.* My shiatsu teacher always said that our bodies will break before our minds or spirits do. So if our sexual energy dries up, it may have a physical cause. But it may also be just our unwillingness to allow our partners to see us fully. Both partners need to be committed to passion with one another — in the same way they are committed to personal growth or the longevity of marriage. This way lies untold delight!

The easiest way out of a relationship is to fall in love with someone new. "Get a new horse, ride out of town!" What a sloppy way of refusing to do the honest work needed for growth! There may come a time when it is inappropriate to be together. But that is a decision that should not rest simply on your sexual attraction to — or distraction with — another. Reflective, respectful work is what is demanded of your decisions to enter into or to dissolve a wedding covenant.

What Is the Long View?

Marriage and commitment are to be taken very seriously. Their greatest rewards are not short-term. When my mother was diagnosed with breast cancer in her seventies — some fifty years into her marriage, she was very clear that it was in Dad's love and support that she could rest her fears. If you let it, the heady pleasure of romance can become the solid foundation needed for raising children and facing life's ups and downs. Throughout your married life, the bass note of companionship will deepen and strengthen, if you but let it. Your passion for one another can only be maintained and intensified by your willingness to remain open and committed to one another.

If at some crisis point you decide you can't continue to live together, then you will need to know that what you have done has been worthwhile and valuable. I believe that your chances of staying together are much greater if you know and remember all the wonderful things about who you are together.

If you've decided to have children, you need to have a firm commitment to stay together. So you need to be very sure as you make the decision to welcome children that you're in a marriage you can live in. I don't mean to say that people need to stay in dangerous or demeaning situations for the sake of the children. I do mean to say you should not have children if your relationship is dangerous or demeaning. Both of you need to be committed to doing what it takes to make a secure home for your children. Make your relationship a reason for marriage that your children will point to with pride.

While a good divorce ceremony can acknowledge and help you move on from your promises, it can't erase the fact that you made them. In the wedding ceremony you are saying your integrity lies in your relationship with this person. Marriage is finding a way to be committed and faithful to your integrity.

What I wish for you, what I wish for every married couple, is that you may stand together at your children's wed What I wish for you, what I wish for every married couple, is that you may stand together at your children's wedding, or a parent's funeral, your beloved's retirement, or some other significant event thirty years in the future and know that you have worked hard on your relationship; that the seeds you sowed on your day of commitment have grown into something substantial and beautiful. If you have taken your promises to one another seriously — even if you are no longer married — you should be able to stand next to one another at those important events and look back with great pride, saying, "What a good thing we did together!"

Chapter 2
Why Not Elope?

There is nothing that says you can't just stand up at dinner and make an informal announcement that from now on you and your sweetie will be living together as a family. However, most often the response to that would be, "Why, how lovely, dear. Would you pass the gravy?"

Your wedding is a celebration of your loving partnership before those people who mean the most to you. You can make it an invitation to your community to understand how your relationship transforms and challenges you. A wonderful gift that can come from a public wedding is that you can begin to comprehend your community's real support for you and your promises. This support is something you can call on as you move forward in your life together. You will want to claim that support for the raising of your child. You will want it when a family member is ill or someone close to you dies. You will want it as you make hard decisions about your career or life path. You will want it when marriage is more difficult than it is on this most glorious of days.

Ritual allows you to make yourself heard, and it allows your community the opportunity to reflect on your words and to offer you their support in a formal setting. It allows you to celebrate something that's really important to you:

this wonderful, fulfilling, challenging, loving relationship with your partner. Taking time out, setting it apart, to tell your community what you feel and what you believe, creates a space in which people listen differently.

The purpose of ritual or ceremony is to celebrate the way people live. It supports and clarifies the values which form us and helps us to make meaning of our lives. Ritual has power and creates the time and space in which we can be deliberate about our actions. Through ritual you can allow your wedding ceremony to say clearly, to all involved, what your plans are for becoming family to each other. It used to be that the institutions of church and society defined family for us, but this is no longer true. Since there are no over-arching traditions or institutions for many of us, this is the first time we have had to accept responsibility for our futures on our own terms.

The wedding ritual and the promises you make within it can become the trellis on which you will plant the vine of your relationship, something to support you and your relationship when times are troubled.

A wedding ceremony that is a guide for growth will leave you with clear reminders about why you chose to enter into marriage with this person and will help you to stay present and involved when you're in the middle of a blazing argument.

Remembering the love and commitment you celebrated on your wedding day is a way of returning to where you started and allowing yourself to see both how love has grown and flourished, and where you may have neglected your promises to be lifelong partners in love. Of course you can have a good marriage without a personalized wedding ceremony. But you can *use* this ritual to establish the precedent for honesty and openness in your marriage, and it can do nothing but help your relationship thrive.

What Ritual Does

The several-fold purpose of ritual at its best: it

∞ gathers our communities together to support our individual tasks,

∞ separates us from the day-to-day existence of our lives and creates sacred space to reflect upon our lives,

∞ allows us to examine the structure and actions of our lives,

∞ provides an opportunity for us to tell our truth and our intentions, and

∞ asks our community to hear us.

With no other place to discuss and review our lives with our communities, the deliberate creation of ritual allows us to re-establish the sacred, celebrate the incredible abundance of life and share our understanding of what is meaningful with our communities. Today's ritual actions must be far more explicit and deliberate than yesterday's so that the gathered community can make meaning of the ceremony that is taking place before them. A crucial element of ritual is the way it joins individuals into a community that can acknowledge, honor and strengthen our deepest sense of humanity. Ritual actions performed today can become the basis for creating new ritual actions within the community.

What Ritual Isn't

When we talk about ritual, we immediately think of the ordinary "rituals" that we indulge in every day. Most of those will prove to be habits or routines. For instance, every morning, I wash my hair before I wash my body. I don't feel clean if I don't start with my hair. And I can't do either of those things if I haven't brushed my teeth. Starting my day in a prescribed way sets me up for a good morning.

However, no matter how insistent and how comfortable I am about my routine, it doesn't add meaning to my life. My community of friends and family might order their morning ablutions very differently, and this will have very little effect on my life. This series of morning activities is not a ritual.

Public Ritual Changes Lives

I believe absolutely that rituals change lives. In an opening conversation with me, many couples will say, "We've been living together for years. A wedding ceremony won't really make any difference." And then we go through the process of planning and clarifying, and they get married. A year later, I'll receive a note or a call, and the couple will rave about the differences in their lives since they made that public commitment.

What you say, in public, in a structure that allows you to be seen as you see yourselves, makes a difference in the way you treat each other and in the way your community treats you and your relationship. Your friends will take this seriously. This is a good thing. It means, however, that you had better be careful to say exactly what you mean.

A Safe Environment for You

Ritual creates a safe environment within which you can risk sharing your inmost self with your community.

The importance of this is not to be underestimated.

Committing yourself to a lifetime in your partner's company is scary. It doesn't matter how sure you are that you are making the right decision; it doesn't matter how precisely you've planned and prepared — getting married is a big deal. It should be! There's very little else in our lives that we commit to for a lifetime. The way in which you marry your partner must provide as much comfort and structure to lean on as possible to enable you to concentrate on the life-changing commitment you're making.

Well-articulated ritual, presided over by a person who is familiar with the process and responsible for it, can assist the community in opening to what you have to say. It's helpful to know what kind of ritual the majority of your community members are used to. What are they expecting and how do you deal with their expectations? Clarity on this is invaluable so that you can let them know what will fit and not fit their preconceptions. Tell people what they're going to experience that they're not expecting, and tell them what they're not going to experience that they might have been expecting. This helps the community prepare for what will happen during the ceremony.

A wedding ritual should help the community members remember their own promises and remind them of the importance of commitments. It should help the listeners open to hear the words of the participants. To do this, you need to provide safe space for the community as well as for the couple. Using ritual actions that are familiar to the community can reassure people. Words and concepts that they associate with wedding ceremonies will open space for the new ideas you're bringing in. You don't want to use language or activities simply because they've always been used. You want to use things with meaning for you. The repetition of the old helps your community to relax into the new.

Marriage has evolved, but the vows and ceremonies used by religious institutions for centuries have not adapted to the multiplicity of ways in which people now live as life partners. There is value in saying words that our parents and grandparents said: the language of covenant must be weighty and well thought out. However, for promises to have meaning, they should be based upon the realities of the partners' lives and relationship, and phrased in the language of today.

Ritual and Community

Ritual has a communal base even when it is an individual activity. Our lives make sense and have meaning within the context of our community's understanding of what is important. The easy familiarity of shared life or community, which led to shared meaning, has disappeared along with neighborhoods and parishes. It is up to us to begin to build new concepts of community that include and embrace the people we rely on in our day-to-day lives.

Today, our communities are those people who know us, those people with whom we share an understanding of what is valuable. There are friends from childhood, friends from high school, friends from university, friends from our jobs, friends from our interests. Frequently these cohorts do not overlap and often we leave groups behind, at least geographically, as our lives change. We are not in daily contact with one another, although we stay in touch by letter, phone and e-mail. We don't live in the same neighborhoods and gossip on the front porch or over the back fences. Our kids don't grow up running in and out of each other's houses. We don't share our spiritual traditions or participate in organized religious groups that create communities with shared meaning with our partners or our friends.

Communities today are much more widely spread out, sharing neither geographic proximity nor faith traditions. Just as many people describe their romantic life as serial monogamy, serial communities are often the norm today. Also, in this time in history, our lives are defined in both secular and individual terms; the workplace and school have replaced the church as the centers and the delineators of human existence. There were many different churches in old town centers, and the focus of those churches was the spiritual well-being of the individuals and the communities with which they were entrusted.

The workplace is directed towards profit. That's its mission. While we may make good friends at work, our job there is to help the company, and therefore ourselves, prosper. It is not to establish a safe place to raise children or to care for the elderly or to build our emotional home in a group of like-minded people.

It helps our communities when we clarify our relationships with them and with one another. We have to do the work to allow them to see the connections and the support that make life so rich. They need to know that however loosely tied we are, we live our lives within the boundaries of our love for one another.

How do we communicate this? How do we create communal meaning in our lives if we don't all live together? What do we celebrate if we don't all believe the same things? What do we do with the ancient ceremonies and rituals that don't really speak to our lives? We long for familiar forms to link us to the past and at the same time long for new words to reflect who we are today and what we hope to become. It is not only the coming together around a special occasion that gives meaning, but it is the repetition of those events within a community that allows them to be recognized.

What Is Meaning? Why Does It Matter?

Your wedding is an opportunity to establish a precedent within your community of making explicit that which too often goes unmentioned: your love for someone, your hopes for your career or your children, your grief at someone's passing. Saying who you are and what you wish to accomplish with your life is a way of establishing meaning in your life. You explain what you value and how you wish to live. You acknowledge the importance of your connection to specific individuals and to your gathered community. In this way, you offer people an opportunity to learn from you and act to bring their own meaning into their community of support. Your wedding can become a legacy of meaning-sharing within your community. This is a gift you can give yourselves and your community by designing a ritual that celebrates your life.

You Are a Part of This Community

Mark yourself as a part of your community by using parts of rituals that your family or friends have used in their weddings. As the community recognizes the ritual action, this ties you into your community. Using a ring that was worn by elders during their long and happy marriage or reading a poem or a piece of scripture that has been read at every family wedding will remind the community of your place in their lives.

Meg and Sheila asked their friend Sam to read a blessing

29

at their wedding. We ended the ceremony by singing a song that had been sung at Sam's commitment ceremony many years before. Sam and her partner were touched to have their service remembered. The rest of us honored the courage that these women had needed to proclaim their commitment thirty years before. Thus Meg and Sheila established their place in the stream of women who have proclaimed their love. What a wonderful thing!

Design Adaptable Ritual

Kara and David's brother, Peter, had baked their wedding cake. We designed a small ritual for the reception that took the sharing of cake and sweetness as a serious obligation, one that was equal to the obligation of nurturing and understanding. When the cake was cut, the bride and groom offered cake to one another and then invited each of us to share in the sweetness of their lives. Each of the guests then offered cake to a neighbor, symbolically refusing to keep the best for themselves. When Peter died several years later, we celebrated the cake ceremony at his memorial service, taking communal meaning from what we had done together in a different context. When Kara's younger brother Dave married Julie, we celebrated with cake and remembered again how sweetness sustains and develops us.

The Place

Choose a place for the ceremony where you feel called into the best of who you both are.

Many of the couples I marry are looking for an outside environment because that is where they connect with their spirituality. Others choose a small and intimate restaurant because hospitality and intimacy are the hallmarks of their relationship with themselves and with others. Or a couple will know that a building with a view over the city is the only fit setting for their marriage.

While you can always justify your choice once you've picked a place, it's important to have your criteria together before you begin to look. In this way your wedding is much more likely to be what you had always envisioned.

Allow your concept of "home" or "religious/spiritual" sites to expand to include this place where you will be gathering. You can make an impersonal place part of your personal history by claiming it and calling in those things that are important to you in that space. Picking the place where you'll be married is important.

The Rehearsal

Most people think the rehearsal is held so that people can practice walking in and walking out. And certainly that's helpful. It's always amazing to me how nervous attendants get about walking down the aisle — and they're not even getting married! Generally I will get everyone in place and review the ceremony and then let people practice walking out and in. That way people know where they're coming to and going from.

But the real purpose of the rehearsal is to remind the crowd what is really happening during the ceremony. This is not merely a performance for bride, groom and attendants. This is an important milestone in the life of two people.

Outlining the ceremony and reviewing the importance of the community and family witness and participation in the life of these two people helps everyone remember the importance and the solemnity of this event.

Attendants have been chosen because they are your closest friends and family. Their job is to support and encourage the two of you. The best thing they can offer you that day is their absolute focussed attention.

I always remind people that alcohol interferes with people's ability to be present and I ask everyone not to drink before the ceremony. I remind attendants that they are there to run interference on all the silly decisions people will want you to make. I've had people call the bride two hours before the wedding to ask what they should wear. As if it were her problem!

Your job that day is being fabulous and being in love. The attendants' job is to help you shine. The rehearsal is the place to review that.

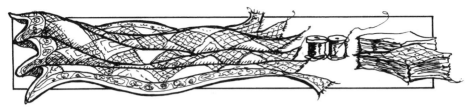

Chapter 3
Crafting Your Ceremony

Good ritual has purpose. The purpose of a wedding ritual is to invite the community to witness and bless the promises that a couple makes to one another. Good ritual also has a beginning, a middle and an end. Without that flow, the ritual doesn't work for either the participants or the observers.

I've researched the ritual texts from many traditions, trying to figure out the important elements of ritual. From this research, I've developed an outline of the essential elements of a wedding. If you follow this outline, tailoring the pieces to your life and your relationship and using any of the small ceremonies that have meaning in your life or appeal to you, this should enable you to create a meaningful and beautiful wedding that people will talk about for years to come. More importantly, it will help you make a loving commitment to your life partner that will be supported by your community. That's a successful wedding ceremony!

Your wedding is a time to invite people into your lives and to tell them what is important to you as individuals and as a couple. This is inevitably a time when differences between generations and families will surface, so you want to look for ways to make people comfortable with those differences. Expressing yourselves in a straightforward and heartfelt way will allow people to hear you, even through their differences, especially if you have constructed a ceremony that invites people to really listen to you. There are plenty of wonderful things that you can do to reassure and allow your community whole-hearted participation in your ceremony without sacrificing your integrity or the personal meaning of your ceremony.

Introduction / Invitation

The Introduction or Invitation describes why this group has gathered, who invited them, what will happen and what will be asked of each party during the ritual. It includes a discussion of the couple, your decision to marry and the promises you will make. It calls your community together to witness your covenant, and explains what commitments you will ask of the community. If you are doing things that are not traditional in the entire community for a wedding ceremony, it mentions those elements. People have a much better time if they are aware of what's going to happen.

In this very secular society, many people are unclear of ritual's purpose, so it is helpful to remind people of the role and nature of ritual in their lives. If you believe, as I do, in the power of ritual to transform lives, it is important to explain what is intended in this particular ritual. Remind the audience that ritual is an outgrowth of a community's changing experience and does not have a static nature. Good ritual is reflective of what people believe and how they live.

The Invitation can explain the need to transform rituals that are archaic and obsolete. This is a delicate point to be approached with great reverence for the original tradition.

34

In that way, people can appreciate both the need to reclaim ancient rites and have them evolve and change so that they have special meaning for the wedding couple.

Each ritual has a history that must be respected. Explain why it has meaning for you and how you are transforming it. In this way, the ritual becomes yours and also begins to shape the entire community's understanding. Be very cautious about using the rituals of other peoples. Far too often, we are very casual about adopting ritual activity from traditional societies, paying little regard to either that culture's history or their willingness to share their ritual. Some ritual cannot be incorporated easily into other traditions. Appropriate ritual is that which has historical context within your own family or community, whether that be your community of birth or your community of choice.

For instance, when using the chuppa as a symbol of hospitality, it helps to remember that, today, couples participate much more equally in the provision of the home and in the domestic acts that care for the home and the family that dwells there. In light of these altered roles, it becomes important to discuss the changes and the impact they have on the ritual. Where ritual excludes or demeans, it must be opened to include and exalt. In this way people are transformed from observers to participants.

To symbolize the movement toward joint participation in the creation and sustenance of the home, Valenta made their chuppa covering from old shirts and skirts and fabric that had been important to Mark and her. They planned to use this cloth in their bedroom after the wedding as a canopy or a quilt cover. In this way they personalized and deepened the meaning for this part of the ritual. So much sweeter than renting their chuppa, it also made a statement that both the

Jewish side of the family and the non-Jewish side of the family could comprehend. Because we explained the creation of the canopy at the beginning of the ceremony, Mark and Valenta's thoughtful action created meaning for their community.

The Invitation should end with a welcome from the couple to the gathered community that moves the ceremony toward the Invocation.

Invocation

To invoke means to "call upon." During the Invocation I call on at least two things: the space we are inhabiting and the community who are the witnesses. Dependent upon the couple's spiritual lives and references, I will also invoke Spirit or God. The ritual will take place and the transformation of two single people into a covenanted pair will happen. Therefore this is what must, with the community's consent, be made holy or intentional.

Ritual Space. I work mostly with people who do not have a faith community or are marrying across traditions. My weddings take place in hotels and restaurants, and because I live in a temperate climate, many are performed outside. This means that space needs to be set apart for the ceremony. Houses of worship are consecrated spaces; the space is used regularly for sacred ritual action. In other places, space needs to be consecrated by and dedicated to the actions we take there. If a couple has chosen to be outdoors because they have an affinity with nature, or with this particular environment, then the community needs to understand and appreciate that affinity. During the Invocation it must be said that this place is special and set apart for this ritual action in this point in time.

The work we are about to undertake here is sacred and holy and echoes the actions of our ancestors and their ancestors who came together in love. You and I, as participants and observers, join the cloud of witnesses from generations gone by who have made room for love to flourish. Today, let us acknowledge that friends, joined together in celebration, create a sacred circle.

David and Amy have chosen to call their community together in this simple and beautiful place because nature and community are essential elements of their life. They have chosen to make their promises in the shadow of this grand old tree. Trees have been symbols of life for many religious communities. Trees nurture and shelter us. Their roots reach deep into the earth and their branches push boldly into the sky. It is said that the roots of a tree are as great as the branches and thus offer us a wonderful sense of balance. Left alone, they will flourish for many years, utilizing all the forces of nature as they grow.

What a wonderful metaphor for the powers of life and love! Today this tree also serves as a natural chuppa. A chuppa is always a piece of a Jewish wedding ceremony. Today in this place David remembers his Jewish heritage and he remembers all his ancestors who have stood beneath a canopy to make their promises to one another. Therefore, let us say that this place is special and that our intentions are good.

The Unbroken Circle. Often our families and friends have not met. They may have heard all about each other and know histories and backgrounds, but this might be the first face-to- face meeting for each other's childhood friends and college buddies. It may be that the couple is about to move so that they will be saying goodbye to a part of their life and their community. This is such a mobile society that it's too often unclear who the larger community is. Sometimes they are family members getting together for the first time in several decades. But here, all together at last, ready to celebrate friends' or families' lives, it is important to take a moment to look around and notice the people seated here.

They are the larger community that is called upon not only in times of celebration, but also in times of stress. Therefore it is good to recognize one another as allies in the lives of friends and families. Ask the community to say hello to one another — either in a communal response, or if the gathering is small enough, invite the community to greet one another personally. (In Christian tradition, this personal greeting is known as "Passing the Peace.")

Because in most cases this is not a community that worships together on a regular basis, we want to agree that our intentions are good, or holy, or sacred.

> Notice all who are gathered here today; let us
> call upon all those who are with us in spirit only,
> and let us say to one another: Peace and greetings
> to all.

What Do You Believe? While these first two elements of my Invocation are always present in some form, the next element is dependent upon the spiritual lives of the wedding

38

couple and their communities. Is it to be a religious ceremony? Is a spiritual ceremony different from a religious ceremony? Is the couple atheist or agnostic? Be clear about the celebrant's spiritual life and belief system and whether or not he or she can work outside it if it's not closely aligned with yours.

My friend Doug, a Baptist minister, believes that his authority to marry people comes from his position in the church. He celebrates Christian ceremonies that facilitate a couple's being enfolded in Christian community. Another friend who is an Episcopal priest marries only those who belong to her community. As long as you are not asking me to say things that are contrary to my beliefs, I will follow your wishes on the inclusion of God or Spirit in your ceremony.

This is your wedding ceremony, and it should reflect your belief systems. Each person's viewpoint is necessary and must be represented. Some people will be married into the Christian Church, or the Jewish, Buddhist or Islamic traditions; some will not. Some may wish to have prayer; some may wish just to have mention of spiritual connections. For the couple, asking and answering these questions presents a wonderful opportunity for a clarifying conversation about each partner's beliefs and how to include them in the ceremony (or exclude them).

Below are some approaches to invoking a blessing. Various clients and I wrote all the text.

> *Community Blessing* We give thanks today for the
> gift of love which calls this couple ever more deeply
> into their relationship. We ask a blessing on them
> as they reaffirm their willingness to take the risks

of loving well and moving beyond their fears. May they accept the challenge to be ever more fully themselves, more fully with each other and more fully a part of those around them. Bless them, and bless us all. Blessed be.

Alcoholics Anonymous   All knowing Spirit, Higher Power, join us in this ceremony binding the lives and destinies of these two lovers. We ask a blessing on this couple, on their marriage and on the life they will lead together. As they speak and we hear the words that will forever join them, allow the intentions being uttered to remain true through time and to run as deep as a singing river throughout the landscape of their lives.

Christian   Let us pray: Sweet and Holy God, we are here today to witness and bless this marriage. Hold them in the palm of your hand as they venture out into the unknown, trembling yet sure. Help them to remember that it is in the void that the miracle of life occurs. Create within them bold and passionate hearts for all that lies ahead. Bless those of us who are gathered to support them and bless them as they embark on their new life together. We pray this in the name of Jesus, our brother. Amen.

Spiritual   Sweet and Holy Spirit, you are strong in this place and in our hearts. We give thanks today for the gift of creation and the forces that move the world. We give thanks for all of the beautiful spaces that move us beyond ourselves. We give thanks for the love that grows and flourishes where once there was nothing. We ask a blessing on this couple, on their marriage and on the life they will lead together. As we offer them our support and good wishes, let us remember the promises we keep and let us be glad for one another. Blessed be.

Joining Your Families

Different things are now true about families joined by marriage than were true just twenty years ago. Neither family relinquishes a child to the other family. Rarely will the new couple live with, or even in close proximity to, one set of parents. We often live far away from our families of birth, so if there are cousins, they will play together only at family reunions. The ties that hold the extended family together are much looser than they were in times past.

The bride and groom are adults joining their lives. They are represented by their parents, who welcome the creation of this small family unit and a new family member as their child's partner. *The families are also forming a relationship, however informal, with their child's partner's family.* So when there are celebrations, both sides of the family converge to mark the occasions. With today's marriages, we truly don't lose children to other families but gain new family associations. It is more and more common to find in-laws becoming friends and tangling the family lines into a lovely mess.

It is up to your families to decide how friendly or frequent those meetings will be, but this is another opportunity to recognize the allies who offer support as you live your lives. During the ceremony I always ask if the two families understand the bond being made between them. Then I remind them of the supportive and celebratory roles they will play in the couple's life.

This is very important. I preface these questions with some commentary on the fact that it is in our families, of birth and of choice and of spirit, that we learn about love. This is as true for what we know about healthy love as for what we know about dysfunctional relationships. Our willingness to risk joining our lives together is testimony to the successful models of marriage we have known. We may cherish what we had in our families, and we may mourn what we missed at home and saw at a neighbor's home. What's important is that the couple express their gratitude for the love they have known.

> Julie and David come to this ceremony today as adults making a free choice to join their lives together. Their love for each other is grounded in the love they enjoy and share with their family and friends. We are reminded that this marriage is not only a celebration of the family they are creating but also a thanksgiving for their families of birth and spirit who have loved them. And so I ask today, Who comes here with David to welcome Julie to their family?
>
> *We do.*
>
> Who comes here with Julie to welcome David to their family?
>
> *We do.*
>
> Are you two families willing to acknowledge the bond that this marriage makes among you? And are you willing to share together all that lies ahead?
>
> *We are.*

Statement of Intent

This and the Statement of Support are the heart of my wedding ceremonies. Ceremonies are more memorable when couples are willing to talk about their lives and their love for one another. Strangely enough, this is not part of most ceremonies. *It took me a while to realize people rarely say "I love you" in their own voices in their wedding ceremonies.*

This section can be tricky. Don't feel it needs to be the most complete explanation of love and relationship that will ever be written. It's really just a snapshot of what you value in one another and your relationship.

I have developed a worksheet to help you formulate what you can say to one another during your wedding. Write it down and share it with one another and your celebrant. Then you have your words to refer to as you go through life together. Find the worksheet in the appendix on page 105.

People tell stories about how they met or what they like to do together. Others simply recount those things that make this a remarkable relationship in their life. Comfort, respect, safety, passion, humor — the list is endless. What's most important is that what you write should sound like you: "This is what is true about the person that I love. This is why I believe that we have a lifetime ahead of us."

This vision of your relationship gives you something to refer to, something to fall back on. Couples laugh when I say that this is a great piece of paper to haul out if you should reach a point in the future where you wonder why you ever married.

"But it says here that you *like* that part of me!"

"I was infatuated," the partner might respond!

Anne and Jim wrote very touching Statements of Intent.

Anne said in her statement that she cherished making pancakes on Sunday mornings with Jim and looked forward to a lifetime of Sunday mornings doing that with him and their family. It was so easy to see them in a sunny yellow kitchen growing old together. It was a satisfying and hopeful image to take away. She also mentioned her fear of the dentist and confessed that Jim took the time to drive her to the dentist and make her sing silly songs on the way and that that time together was totally transforming in their relationship. One: he understood her fear and didn't try to embarrass her out of it. Two: he responded in a really productive way. Jim had equally sweet things to say about Anne. These word pictures really allowed all of us to know what there was between them and what they were committing to protecting and enriching.

Toni Morrison says in *Beloved*, "The only grace you can have is the grace you can imagine. If you can't see it, you can't have it."

We need to dare to imagine what we want in life. Without that vision, it is unlikely we'll get there. How many couples got married in the late '60s and '70s for as long as love lasted? You know what? Love lasted until the first really big bump came along.

Relationships are unlikely to last sixty years unless they are specifically dedicated to a lifelong process. It is not — as many can testify — a particularly easy process. So if you're going to work toward that goal, why not say so and gather the support you'll want to get there?

Promises made for a lifetime can and do endure. So say what you want to say to one another in your own words. Don't just parrot words that someone else wrote for "every couple." When you make your promises in your own words, you know what to do to make those promises last. Act respectfully and respectably in designing and living the relationship about which you are exchanging promises. I see too much bad behavior from families or divorced parents. I really want to help you establish what is good and wonderful about this relationship so that you can call on it when times are tough. Whatever your marital status thirty years from now, you will have made these promises to each other, with all the wholeness you could bring to your life at this time.

In the appendix on page 105, there is a worksheet that will help you to establish a framework for writing your Statement of Intent. The final statement can either be culled from phrases you write there, or this sheet can merely be used as a launching pad. Either way, it can be most helpful.

Statement of Support

This is not an easy time in which to make marriage work. Career demands, caring for children and aging parents, health and exercise activities all have assumed roles of major importance — sometimes to the point that the relationship gets buried by life's demands. We are among the most individual and independent people who ever lived. Our ability to make it on our own is an important hallmark of our success as individuals. Finding a balance between our needs as individuals, our responsibilities as adults, and our duties as life partners is a difficult and challenging task. And let's not forget that parenting thing! Life-long commitment happens only when the couple works diligently at lifting up the relationship and its importance to them.

However easily families and family values are talked about, very little today supports families and intimacy. We are not comfortable when our friends are "mushy," which is often how we interpret sincere declarations of love. Fight in front of us, and we can gossip about that forever. We'll take sides or judge or just enjoy the discomfort. But, ask us to bear witness to the profound changes that loving a particular someone makes in your life, and we're as uncomfortable as if you chose to show us your appendectomy scar at the dinner table.

But we've come together at your wedding to celebrate your relationship. What's important in this world? Many people easily agree love is a fundamental value for a meaningful life. But it's rarely said aloud — even in a wedding ceremony. When do we hear people say, "I love you, and I want to spend the rest of my life with you?" Very infrequently! And yet, the profession of love is a transforming event. I know this because of the large numbers of people who have been witnesses at my weddings who tell how touched they were to hear declarations of love, how it moved them to offer declarations of love to those who were most important in their lives.

Communities play a vital role in supporting us as we make and maintain commitments. What we ask of our community on our wedding day is symbolic of what we wish from them our entire lives:

∞ Hear us when we talk about our dedication to being good lovers and partners.

∞ Remind us of the privilege and wonder of committed relationship as we struggle with all the little pieces in our lives.

∞ Support us in our integrity as we agonize over the daily decisions to remain in partnership.

Having been asked to hear our vows and our intentions,

our communities have a responsibility throughout the course of our married life to remind us that we made those vows with an open heart and now must keep our hearts open as we struggle to find a way to live them out. This is why we invite people to our wedding. Not simply to celebrate today, but to keep faith with us as we journey through our life together. As the wedding ceremony is a momentary action in the work of a lifetime, so is the promise to support and nurture the family.

So at each wedding I celebrate, after the couple speaks about why they are marrying, I offer the community an opportunity to make a choral response of support to the couple. When the couple has really risked opening their hearts to their community with the statement of intent, the group will want a way to respond to this gift of trust. Therefore, after I talk about communal responsibility to relationship, I will ask the community to repeat a phrase such as this one:

> Tom and Cindy, we are witnesses of your intentions, and we pledge you our support.

After the couple's words of intention, the crowd is eager to speak up in support. The wave of emotion can be almost tangible because the crowd is so engaged in what is happening. Couples who have had these words said to them look forward to having the opportunity to say them to the next couple to be married. I run into people in a grocery store or on the street who attended a wedding I performed, and they want to tell me how well the couple is doing — or that they never miss sending them anniversary cards. In one case where over time I had married three couples in a crowd of friends, the first couple was getting a divorce by the time the third couple was marrying. The second and third couples came to me, visibly upset. "What should we do? We made them a promise and they won't even talk about it." It was disconcerting for them to realize that there was no way to preserve vows that the community had taken seriously. It underlined for me how important an action this is.

In the past I have asked the guests of smaller weddings to come with wishes or prayers to offer the couple. After two rather disastrous occasions, I now council my couples to consider very carefully if they want wishes to be spoken aloud by the communities. On both occasions, the couples were very surprised by the religiosity of some of their guests — guests they thought they knew very well. Both times these guests managed to have the last word. The atmosphere and the mood of both these weddings were really changed by the wishes, and the couples felt uncomfortable.

Now, I suggest they collect wishes in a keepsake bowl or book that the couple will treasure throughout their relationship. The guests' words are gathered, and the couple still retains some control over the theology!

I see this section of the wedding as one where a core piece of work is done as the community accepts its role as supporters and nurturers of marriage.

Images of Relationship

There are a lot of places in the wedding ceremony where art forms can really enhance the ritual. A wedding ritual is strong enough to stand alone and does not need filler. There is no need to have poetry or music or dance in your wedding ceremony if they have no meaning in your life.

That said, the possibility exists for music, poetry and dance to really transform an event. If the work has meaning for the couple or the community, if there are words or music or movement that impart a transcendent message or deepen the community's participation, then by all means, find them. If there is an artist who belongs to the community and who is available to perform, then that work can make a ceremony come alive.

If you use art forms in your ceremony, it's important to have them performed by someone capable. There is nothing more frustrating than listening to a good poem badly read by someone who can't project and doesn't have a real feeling for poetry. Songs sung by the wrong people can be endless. More than once in the midst of an endless vocal performance, either by a community member or a professional, my couples became bored and nervous, and began to fidget or talk. I have had to tell wedding couples to quiet down in the midst of the second bridge of a four-stanza song. Let me tell you, it doesn't add to the ceremony!

Dan and Michelle, both actors, wanted the directions called in and they asked some of their theater buddies to participate in this. Two people were there for each direction. One person read the invocation and another laid an appropriately colored ribbon on the floor to form a circle for the couple to stand in to get married. It was dramatic, beautiful and very effective.

At one wedding, quite a few of the groom's friends were actors, and John and Melissa both had strong ties to poetry. They asked several people to read the work of poets who ranged from personal friends to national treasures. The impact of beautiful verse, beautifully read was astounding. The whole community was transfixed. Similarly, vocalists have offered songs in such a way that the meaning of the poetry and the music were made available to everyone. Hoary chestnuts in the hands of accomplished performers suddenly reveal what their composers intended them to say! I've been to enough weddings where *Evergreen* or *Sunrise, Sunset* were sung that I have no great desire to hear them ever again. Yet at one wedding, a friend of the bride performed both of them with great poise and meaning. The whole crowd cried. (Even I cried, and I work very hard at not doing that at wedding ceremonies!) The wedding ceremony can introduce the use of community art and artists as an integral part of communal events. Tears all around, and what a good thing that is at a wedding ceremony!

Dance is also a phenomenal addition if the artist knows how to incorporate it into the community experience. At one wedding, as people arrived, they were given paper and pen and asked to write wishes for the couple. In the middle of the ceremony a dancer collected those wishes in a silver vessel as she danced. The dance added color and movement and allowed the community another opportunity to participate in the ritual. Another time, a liturgical dancer led the entire group in some simple movements that transformed the Taize chant *Oh Lord, Hear My Prayer.*

Community participation in ritual can be transformative. As your friends and family take part in your ceremony, they participate in the idea of your relationship and recognize the importance of the role they play in your life.

People are honored to help you. People like to sing together. People like being inspired. Some people in your community will love creating ritual; some people just want to show you how much they love you. This makes their promise to support you and your relationship a tangible, comprehensible thing. Community participation in the ceremony underscores the Statement of Support by your community.

There are a number of really good books out which offer poetry choices for weddings. Good bookstores, local libraries and the Internet all offer excellent resources for poetry, prose and music that's appropriate to weddings. I'm not a very romantic person, so the poetry I keep leans toward the deep and meaningful rather than hearts and flowers, but each person who performs ceremony will have different resources. Many couples have also told me that reading poetry and prose has been a good way to prepare for writing their own Statements of Intent.

Charge to the Couple

Here the celebrant can review the gathered wisdom on marriage and say something meaningful and short about the possibilities of living together in love. This can go in many directions. In a religious tradition, a clergy person might talk about the impact of that tradition on a couple's path. This is often the most specific piece of my ceremony, because I speak directly to your life.

It's good to be reminded about individuality. Your individuality is the most precious gift you can bring to your relationship. Your "couple-ness" is wonderful only as it combines, not submerges, your differences. This is not easy. Indeed, these are the very issues that make relationship hard. Having a reasonable partner is lovely — until he or she is being reasonable about that very thing you're passionate about and you're in the middle of a rant. Your partner's spontaneity can be incredibly irritating when you're planning something really important to you that you want carefully orchestrated. It is at these moments that you must struggle with each other's incredible individuality and hope to find that difficult balance in loving relationship. It offers big rewards, but demands big sacrifices.

My colleague Susan often talks about the cycle of life: that there are periods of dormancy which we must live through, that there are buds of promise that may or may not completely develop, and that there are blossoms in full flower. As partners, we live in this garden and have the obligation to tend it.

This is a wonderful place in the ceremony to have an elder whom you respect or a couple who has a great marriage talk about the work involved in making life-long loving possible. It's helpful to have a moment that reflects on what you're doing. If you've done your work for the rest of your ceremony, you should be able to actually hear what's being said to you at this point. Always ask whoever speaks to write his or her words down so that you might have them to read later.

I often talk about the responsibility for passion: giving it house-room and allowing it to grow. Our passion for life and our pursuits is what makes us interesting and human. The need to be supportive in times of stress is often emphasized in marriage ceremonies. However, we don't often talk about the need to laugh and to be physically affectionate and to make love. This space is for that. Underline the fact that marriage is a daily choice to be lover, partner, friend and that a ceremony is simply symbolic of that choice.

Vows

Before you make your vows, reaffirm your choice to marry. Traditional language often uses "to take" rather than "to choose." Marriage is about choosing to do the work. Mere *acceptance* of being married is very different from the day-to-day choice to show up and *live* your commitment to your marriage — however difficult you may find it. You've stated your intentions and heard your community's support and their inspiring images of love or partnership to ground your relationship. Based on this, state your readiness to commit to partnership.

> The oaths you make today are both the culmination and the foundation of a life lived intentionally and with great integrity. Knowing what you know about one another and about the rewards and challenges being married, are you now ready to make your promises to one another?

It is best if the language in this section carries the weight of the ages with it. Use language that is solemn and formal and conveys the importance of what you're saying. "Honor" and "cherish" are words to live by. "Forever and ever," "until death do us part," "as we grow old together" all convey the timelessness that marriage requires. You don't need to make vows that belong to another generation or another mode of marriage, but you want to make promises that honor the fact that so many people have walked this path before you. You want the weight of your words to fill the sacred space you have created for this ceremony. (See page 107 in the appendix for a worksheet.)

> I choose you to be my partner in life. As I promise to love you, I promise to love and honor myself. Share my dreams and allow me to share yours. Challenge and encourage me with love. Help me

to grow and flourish as a person. I will nurture you when you need care and support you when you struggle with change. I will keep faith with you and your deeply held beliefs, believing in you when others may doubt. I will cherish you as we grow old. I will love you for as long as I live, and you will be my heart's companion.

Exchange of Rings

Historically, rings symbolized the exchange of money or dowries in the marriage ceremony. In Jewish tradition, it is after the presentation of rings that the statement is made that "you are consecrated unto me by this." In Filipino weddings, money is poured through both the bride's and groom's hands to fall on a plate below — both a wish that money will flow into their lives and, originally, an acknowledgment that money was being exchanged. In this time frame, the rights and responsibilities of both parties were clearly spelled out.

But traditions change. Meaning mutates. When I was a young and single New Yorker, too often rings spoke not of people's dedication, but rather of their unavailability. At that time, far too many people were being married because it was the thing to do, or because they'd slept with each other. Things were hazy. Some women did not have careers, but stayed home and raised families. Other women did not have families, but worked and made a career. There were way too many affairs. Everybody suffered. For me, the wedding ring's journey from finger to pocket to finger again, as people chose when they wanted to be married, is always symbolic of these trying and difficult times. What does it mean when you take off your ring, except in those instances where rings constitute a danger? Aren't you saying by this action that your commitment is not trustworthy at this point?

I am very hopeful when I talk to people about their wedding rings these days. Often both parties have worn in promise the rings they will wear in marriage. In marriage, they move the ring from one finger to the next. Today's couples are anticipating the pleasure of wearing rings. This is not about wearing the ring of ownership, but about acknowledging joy in accepting this symbol of love. It is not "by this you are consecrated to me," but rather "by this I am consecrated to you."

Proclamation

This section is both an acknowledgment that your lives are changed by the promises you have made and a blessing for the future. One of my most important jobs is to be the person who points you to what's happening. The ceremony is complete. Here, after the vows and rings and the myriad small ritual moments that made this ceremony special, it's important to say, "Wake up! Pay attention. Every legal and spiritual need has been satisfied. Your new life is beginning!"

This is a moment of thresholds: we saw life *this* way; now we see it *that* way. However we have seen this couple up to now, here we acknowledge them as a family. This is a celebrated moment. Each tradition has its own special way of celebrating it: The Jews break a glass; Buddhists sound a gong; some African Americans, Wiccans and the Amish jump the broom. In European traditions, this threshold moment has moved outside the ceremony, but it is remembered as the bride is carried over the threshold.

Threshold moments are too often allowed to go unnoticed. It's important to pay attention to exactly where you are. Is this a moment to reconnect to what you know and believe? A moment to touch base with the person you love, uninterrupted by the wider world? Perhaps a moment where you must engage in any number of the circles of our public life? A magic moment in the movement between two things where life is neither this nor that but is rather becoming and unbecoming? It's possible to catch a glimpse of that wonderful transition.

> In life, doors open and close. We make our choices to enter into or depart. The choice is always ours. Each threshold is a place of magic, where one transitions from one thing to the next. Some thresholds we cross only once. Some we will cross again and again. It is important to pay attention as we move from one space to the next. In marriage, we must hold so many places holy: our place of solitude, our place of deepest communion and our ever-widening circles of community and public. There is risk and safety in each of those places. We must be deliberate about where we are and how we move from one place to the next. We must celebrate both the easy flow from one to the other as well as the sustained movement which allows us our wholeness. This is work of ritual and intention.

Blessing

In traditional religious weddings this is where the Wedding Prayer is found. Most of my clients look for a blessing from their community and from me, as the representative of both spirit and tradition. Sometimes my clients will request *The Apache Wedding Blessing* (available on my website) or another equally lovely blessing. Often they want me to deliver the poem or blessing, but it is not unusual for them to ask either an elder from their families or their community, their matchmaker, or someone who reads well, to deliver the blessing. I have also had the congregation participate in a call and response reading of these blessings. All are lovely options.

The first paragraph in the section below is one I wrote and use in most of my ceremonies. By the time I get to this point in the ceremony, I want something that is very familiar to me. This allows me to speak my words with little or no hesitation and makes it easy for me to maintain eye contact with the community. A client asked me to read the blessing that follows. We were never able to find the source for this blessing. If you know, let me know so that I might attribute these lovely words.

> My friends, we have borne witness to this ceremony of marriage. We know that what was done here today did not start here, but has long been true in their hearts. There is no power greater than the power of love freely offered. Will you please stand while individuals from their community ask a blessing:
>
> May every blessing and grace be yours.
> May your love grow stronger and deeper
> with each passing year.
> May joy and delight fill your home.
> May daily problems not vex you unduly,
> nor the desire for earthly possessions

dominate your lives.
May you have true friends to stay by you in
joy and sorrow.
If you have children, may they return your
love many times over.
With wise and generous hearts, may you
help all who come to you in need of
comfort.
And may you reach a ripe old age together,
content for having lived a life of
goodness and worth.

Before I make the wedding pronouncement, I'll remind
you of your promises and responsibilities to deal lovingly
with one another.

Loving another human being is an enormous undertaking. If at the end of our lives it can be said that we loved
one another well, we should be happy indeed. It is not easy
to constantly take another into account in the living of our
lives — but it is a holy task of which only humans among
the species are capable. This is an appropriate place for a
solemn reminder of the worth and the weight of the promises that you have made to one another over your time together.

And then — *drumroll* — it's time to proclaim your marriage. Most states want the officiant to say that it is by the
power which is vested in them by (God and) the State —
but is that the reality? You are married by the promises you
made which led you to this moment and by the way you
live into those promises. I tell people that by those things,
"You are truly married and may you live happily ever after
in this sacred endeavor." And then you can stomp on some-

thing, jump over something, ring the bell, and kiss. I must admit that I have a preference here for kisses that look as if you truly like each other. No one wants to have to deal with too much passion — but a little is a sweet thing. Pecks on the cheek are rather off-putting.

> Annemarie and Jim, what you have said before God, and before your family and friends, let it be true and valid for the rest of your lives. Go in peace and forgive one another freely. Love each other with open hearts and understanding minds. Open to the respect your partner so generously extends to you. Hold hands, laugh, and make room for love to flourish that you may be sustained while you are apart and that you may always find your way back into the center of your life. By your lives together and by your words today in this ceremony of the heart, you are truly married. May you live happily in each other's company forever and may you blessed be.

Benediction

Many people end their ceremony with the kiss, but that doesn't take into account what the wedding ceremony has done. *As a couple, you came here with your vows already established between you. The ceremony is the opportunity for your community to bear witness to the way this relationship has changed your life.* In that act of blessing, the community has been asked to remember their promises made in love and responsibility. The couple's reminder of the transforming nature of love can serve to reinvigorate the community's oaths. The benediction is an opportunity to charge the community, welcomed into this circle, to remember and celebrate intimacy in life.

After a blessing of the general community and the work of making love manifest in the world with which we are charged, I finish with:

> The ceremony is ended, let the celebration continue, today and for the rest of their lives!

Chapter 4
Rituals from the Heart

Ceremonies of Faith and Family

Religion and cultural heritage are two important gifts in your life. They help you to identify yourself as belonging to a particular clan. This sense of self is a great gift to bring to a marriage.

In those couples where only one partner has a clear sense of their cultural heritage, the other partner can be enormously envious. That envy can often be the catalyst for a couple's establishing traditions for their family. If both partners bring a strong family heritage with them, the couple can choose how to honor their families and their faith traditions in their marriage and in their wedding ceremony. These might be two very different decisions.

History and religious affiliations can create stumbling blocks in the creation of a marriage ceremony. They can make the choice of a wedding celebrant more difficult, but someone who understands you can also open up a ceremony to lovingly reflect each partner's heritage. This can be a wonderful opportunity to proclaim who you are, what you believe, and how you will celebrate your life to your family and friends.

Start out right! Do some decision-making now

concerning the inclusion or exclusion of religious symbols and language. Remind your parents and your grandparents that you value what they taught you, even if you have no wish to follow exactly in their footsteps. These reflections of your history and heritage can make your wedding ceremony as complex and beautiful as you are.

Ritual traditions from your family's past, however, can be the most difficult to incorporate into a wedding which is trying to make sense of a relationship that reflects today. It can be quite challenging to balance the honor you wish to give to your ancestors with the need to remake the ritual in your own or your community's own image. If ritual demeans or excludes, it must be transformed. Transforming the meaning of ritual, while retaining some of the original majesty and sense, is not easy. Yet this is precisely the task you must undertake if you wish to bring your history forward into your life. *You don't want any part of your ritual to place limitations upon your relationships, even to please the people you love the most.* With a little bit of work, you can include ancient traditions with up-dated meanings.

Chuppa

One challenging and memorable wedding had a bride whose family blended New York Jews and Italian Catholics, and a groom whose family blended African-American Baptists and white Friends who had lived communally since the 1960s. We needed to find symbols that would combine the heritage of all these groups and allow everyone to find the meaning behind the actions and objects. The couple chose to have a chuppa, which in the Jewish tradition represents the home that the family will build together (originally, the home that the man would provide for his bride). They covered the chuppa with a Kente cloth that the two of them had bought when they were in Africa together, instead of the traditional family prayer shawl or the more commercial lace or flowers. The four people holding the pillars of the chuppa were representative of the diversity of the families. Two were sisters of the bride and groom, and the other two were the couple's very good friends.

Visually, it was rich and satisfying. More importantly, the community recognized both the effort to include everyone and the possibilities for new and wonderful experience that the cross pollination of culture provided.

Chinese Tea Ceremony

Traditionally, a Chinese bride poured tea in her new husband's house, and her position was established as she poured tea for those who were higher in the family hierarchy and received tea from those who had "lower" status. There are few Chinese Americans who embrace this hierarchy today, yet many long for this ritual which ties them to their ancestors and honors their families. What does the offering of tea really mean to them in the present? It is usually hospitality and gratitude they wish to offer in the serving of tea. When I conduct this ceremony, as the celebrant, I pour the tea for the bride and groom, speaking of the wonderful abundance in the world. Tea could be poured just as easily by the parents, in acknowledgment of their gifts to their children of life and nourishment. The bride then offers tea to her new husband's parents, thanking them for the care of their son and assuring them that they will always find a warm welcome in their house. The groom repeats the action with his new wife's parents. In some cases, the parents respond with red envelopes with money in them, an ancient custom in Chinese weddings.

This short ritual follows a part in the ceremony where each of the families welcome their child's spouse to their family and acknowledge the connection forming between the two families.

Origami Peace Cranes

Cranes have been a symbol of healing in Japanese tradition for a very long time. They came into prominence during this century as a result of a young girl who was stricken with radiation sickness after the 1945 bomb was dropped in Hiroshima. She was told to make one thousand cranes as an offering for her health. She died before she completed them, but her classmates finished them and hung them in strings as a memorial to her. This ritual has been adopted as a memorial to all the Japanese who died as a result of the bomb and its fallout.

Since then, people all over the world have made these cranes for healing, and they have now come to stand for peace as well. They have been incorporated into Japanese-American wedding traditions as a reminder of what Japanese-American families have come through, and as a hope that peace will reign in the world and in the marriage that is about to take place. Traditionally, the bride makes the peace cranes herself.

One of my couples, rather than making the cranes themselves, chose to ask their community — individual friends and family members — to make strings of cranes, which were brought to the wedding to add to a holder that the groom's brother had made. It was a stunning procession: individuals and couples coming up the aisle, trailing strings of origami birds. The finished holder, with all its birds, was tremendously beautiful. Each person had been asked to whisper a wish for good luck and long-lasting love into each bird that was folded. Now the birds hang in their house, and all those wishes flutter on the breeze. This is a piece of the ritual that did not end when the ceremony was over.

It was a very brief activity incorporated into the ritual; but their community had participated in the making of the marriage ritual. It was a successful and effective ritual action, which, when explained to the community at large, added an enormous amount of meaning to the ceremony.

Unity Candle

The Unity Candle is the only real ritual activity that has emerged from the western Christian tradition. Although there are many variations, usually there are two candles on the altar, which are already lit before the ceremony or are lit during the ceremony by the mothers or parents of the bride and groom. These represent the bride and the groom and the families from which each came. Then from the first candles the couple lights a center candle, which represents the new relationship or family that is being created. It is unromantic, not to mention unrealistic, to think that couples will be united as one. It is more accurate to say that marriage makes two people three: the individuals remain and the relationship becomes the third entity of their lives. From now on, decisions will take into consideration the health and happiness of each partner and the relationship. Each of the three — the individuals and the relationship — will have its moment of ascendancy and then another will take priority. This is healthy, as long as decisions are made with awareness of where the sacrifices are being made in each decision.

Do not extinguish your own candles as you light the center candle: all three should remain lit throughout the ceremony. At the end of the ceremony, pack the candles up and take them home and burn them until they are finished. Some couples save them for anniversaries; some couples just burn them whenever they want or need a reminder of the promises they have made.

If you're having an outdoor wedding, consider long and hard if you want the unity candle ritual included. If it's done during the day, the light doesn't show up, so the symbolism is diminished. Candles also can blow out when you're outside. This is a problem — three seconds of symbolic married life is not exactly an auspicious beginning! If you are intent upon doing the candle ceremony, find hurricane globes to protect the flame and use long, windproof matches.

There's another problem with outdoor fire on windy days: one of my brides came very close to setting herself on fire as her veil billowed near the flame. Since then I have been much more insistent about where candles are appropriate. Don't be afraid to skip it if it turns out to be too windy.

If you're getting married inside in a reasonably dark space, the candle ceremony can be quite beautiful. Some families have placed little votive candles around the couple's candles to signify family support. One couple gave votives to everyone and asked them to light those candles during a Statement of Support that the community offered the groom and bride.

In one ceremony, the couple's candles were lit by one of the moms to signify the parents' gift of life. Wendy's family could not be present, so Nanci's mom signaled her acceptance of Wendy as a daughter by lighting both of the candles. Her action really deepened the meaning of the ceremony for everyone. Wendy's parents were happy to be represented in this way and full of joy to know that their daughter was coming into a family that would cherish her. This is what I say during this part of the ceremony:

> Each of us brings our own special light to the world. It is the gift of life and spirit which sustains us. As individuals in a couple you must achieve a delicate balance between the responsibility to pursue your own purpose and the privilege of working with your partner to let your love for one another loose in your lives and in your world. Nanci and Wendy, for many years your light has shone bravely. Now the flame that you light between you will illumine your path and help you find your way to your shared future.

Breaking the Glass

In a traditional Jewish wedding, the groom breaks a glass at the end of the ceremony. There is no one "true" meaning for the glass breaking; one of the wonderful things about Judaism is that most customs have several meanings, and there are as many definitions as there are schools of thought.

A rabbi suggested using light bulbs for breaking: they break easily and make a great sound. I have seen people trying to stomp on shot glasses while the friends who provided them laugh hysterically.

There is a superstition about luck and longevity that says the glass must be broken on the first try. Why court bad luck?

Break something that will break. I know plenty of rabbis who use light bulbs.

Ritual marks rites of passage and celebrates boundary crossings. Ted and Shelley have chosen to symbolize crossing the threshold from singleness into family by breaking a glass as a reminder of Shelley's Jewish tradition. Today, they have stood apart and spoken what was in their hearts, invoking that special place that is theirs alone. But the full expression of our humanity includes many relationships and activities. So joyfully they assume their rightful place in their community and their lives and cross the boundary back to present time and the wonderful party that awaits them. As they do so, they will remember all of the crossings that have shaped their lives and dedicate themselves to noticing the instant of transformation, not just the then and the now, but that miraculous moment in between. May they notice and may they make those moments holy in their lives.

Historically, the man has broken the glass. But they have chosen to break the glass together. From this day forward, all that they build will be composed of pieces of the dreams of both. May their love last for as long as it would take to rebuild a perfect vessel from the pieces of their lives and love that lie represented within this folded cloth. When the proclamation of marriage is given, Ted and Shelley will break the glass to start their new life together.

Binding the Couple Together

In the Congo the mothers wrap the couple in a coverlet which will be placed on their wedding bed. The coverlet comes with the community blessing — and therefore the blessing of the Spirits.

This coverlet ritual made its way into the Filipino Catholic tradition, where a lace covering is pinned around the couple. In India, the woman's sari is knotted to the man's scarf. If anyone saw the movie *Braveheart*, you saw the two principals being married by wrapping the hero's plaid around their joined hands. This is a custom that lingers in many Pagan and Christian Orthodox traditions, which uses rope or the priest's stole to join the couple's hands. A headdress is part of the Greek Orthodox tradition — wreaths are joined as one headdress and placed on the couple's heads. These wreaths are kept and each member of the couple is buried with their piece of the headdress. In these traditions, it is understood that marriage is forever.

Small ritual actions can transform, if just for the moment, a parent's fears about the marriage's resulting in a loss of ethnic identity. Families, particularly if there has been tension about racial, ethnic or religious issues, can see that the couple is struggling with the questions and are not merely glossing over real and important issues. This is one of the goals of a successful wedding ceremony. There is so much that can be done in a wedding ceremony which does not add a lot of time, but which will add a powerful result.

Flower Ceremonies

Here are two lovely examples of families that celebrated the couple with flowers. David and Amy listed qualities they believed their marriage would need to flourish. They then discerned who in their community had the most wisdom in that area and wrote notes asking them to present flowers during the ceremony. To keep things short and moving along, I wrote the presentation statements that were used.

Janice and Sharon followed much the same format. On their wedding day, they put a wonderful vase they had received as a present on their altar at the wedding. At a certain point in each of the ceremonies, people walked up, read their cards, presented their flowers and the flowers were arranged in the vase by one of the attendants. In both cases, the ritual went very smoothly and was quite beautiful. People were so pleased to be honored by the couple and the community.

> *Flower Ceremony I*   In coming together, your love forms a vessel, which if properly maintained, will hold and nurture you and your dreams for the rest of your lives. Now you seek to fill this most wonderful container with qualities to enhance and strengthen your life together. Today, you have asked friends and family members to bring you flowers to represent those qualities. Just as each flower takes on a special meaning for you in this ceremony, the people chosen to present them are representatives of your loving community who offer what is in their hearts. These thoughts of love will decorate your home and your hearts long after the individual flowers are gone. I pray that the vessel of your love may always hold beauty to soften the turmoil which will challenge your life and offer you new opportunities for growth.

Jack: I offer you this orchid. For me this day, it represents excitement and adventure. May your lives be filled with joyous exploration of the world around you, between you and inside you.

Nancy and Dan: We offer you this tulip. For us this day, it represents growth and fulfillment. May your lives be filled with challenges accepted and overcome and learning that leads to wisdom.

Diane and Wayne: We offer you this gladiola. For us this day, it represents patience and understanding. May your lives be filled with the time to reflect and the willingness to see beyond the superficial.

Liz and Robin: We offer you this iris. For us this day, it represents harmony. May your lives be filled with a balance between the abundant and the essential, responsibility and freedom, and an understanding that embraces the incredible diversity of the world.

Cerid and Boyd: We offer you this sunflower. For us this day, it represents joy and happiness. May your lives be filled with shared laughter and hope and the ability to recognize, in even the most serious moments, the absurd and the wonderful — and having recognized, to laugh out loud.

Kim and Cabrina: We offer you this rose. For us this day, it represents everlasting love. May your lives be filled with the challenges of passion and repose in each other's arms and growth in each other's presence.

Flower Ceremony II   Today, friends and family members, as representatives of the larger community, have been asked to place petals in a circle around Cathy and Dave to symbolize the protection and support you offer them. It is fitting that these offerings of love should be beautiful, as the love of our friends is a most wondrous thing. When the ceremony ends, they will step outside this charmed circle and leave it lying under the tree as a tribute to the sacredness of their love and as a symbol of their gratitude for the gifts of nature and the folk who love them.

We wanted to mention "circles" as this is an image we're using a lot today. Rings and flowers and trees and community all offer concentric circles of support and life. Not only do circles offer safety and intimacy on the inside, they also offer opportunities for growth and knowledge where they touch the outside world. The larger the circles, the greater the possibility of interaction with others and the greater the potential for knowledge about ourselves and the world around us. As their community we are their possibilities for support and challenge and laughter — all of which call us more deeply into intimacy with ourselves and with our partners. It is no small work that we do here today.

Instead of using flowers, many variations are possible. People can be offered pieces of paper to write their wishes as they arrive at the ceremony, or they can do it at the reception. One couple had family and friends write wishes on small river stones at the rehearsal dinner, which were then presented at the wedding. The rest of the guests had the opportunity to write wishes on stones at the reception. It was lovely — and such a permanent memento of people's good wishes.

Dedication Ceremonies

Some of you may wish to dedicate your ceremony to those who have died or who, for some other reason, cannot be with you on the day of your wedding. This is a nice way to invoke the presence of those whose absence may be overwhelming. It is my experience that it is better to mention the absence than to ignore it. If a parent or family member has passed on, the day will be colored by that important person's legacy. Better to acknowledge it and have the mention be sweet and expected. That way you can be prepared — and have planned around your emotions.

Some couples wish to acknowledge the experience of their spiritual presence. They know how proud and happy their parents or grandparents would be if they were here, and they invite that joy into the ceremony.

A rite of passage is a time to stop and take stock. Not only do we need to look forward to our future, but we must also look back and see where we have come from. Part of that process is remembering all those who helped us become the people we are today. Absent from this gathering today, but strongly present in the hearts of the participants are Ellen's mother, Kathleen Brand, and Tom's mentor, Sam Walton.

Kathleen's influence on Ellen is remarkable, as Ellen stands for everything that Kathleen taught her family to believe. Ellen lives her life with confidence and passion. This is what Kathleen taught all of you who knew her. She taught you to believe in who you are and in your ability to make a difference in this life. Although Kathleen is not here today, she is truly here in spirit.

Sam always loved and cared for Tom and served as his point of light when he needed direction. Sam led by example. He taught Tom not only the benefits of a positive outlook but also the need to transmit that understanding to others. Even in his absence he influences and blesses this relationship between Ellen and Tom.

These two are sorely missed, but the lessons they taught Ellen and Tom live on in their work and in their lives. Please take a moment to notice all who are gathered here today, and let us remember those who are with us in spirit only.

For others, that's too much. They simply want it acknowledged that there are important people who are not here and that their absence is sorely felt. John and Ted felt that if they were to talk about their mothers, they would not be able to continue with the ceremony. So they mentioned in the program how sorely their moms were missed and had beautiful pots of flowers tied with ribbons sitting on the front seats to represent the beauty of their moms' lives.

Chapter 5
When You Don't Fit the Mold

Second Marriages

Love transforms us! Even when our plans and hopes for love and relationship have gone awry, love calls us back to try again. As the song says, "Love is lovelier, the second time around." While that isn't always true, it certainly can be more meaningful and infinitely more precious. You tried before and lost. And now, in the face of life's lessons, you have found someone who allowed you to believe again.

Some people think it's really inappropriate to talk about the fact that there have been other relationships. But in fact, it is just those other relationships and the lessons that you learned there that allowed you to find the love that is being celebrated today. Let your wedding ceremony be a celebration of the way you have grown into loving this person to whom you are pledging your life and your trust. You don't need to dwell on your past: there are many pieces of your past that are better left there. But don't hesitate to celebrate the wisdom that has brought you to today's event.

Relinquishing Past Promises

Some people are ready to make a commitment to a new relationship without any reference to the past. They were in another relationship, and it ended. They finished their business with that relationship and have no need to review their history. But for others, the long-term commitments to people in the past are something that they choose to acknowledge and explain. I quote below from the wedding ceremony of two women who had both been involved in long-term relationships before. They wished to acknowledge how they had been shaped by those relationships and how their growth as human beings had taken them to a place that made those commitments inappropriate. (Note that in this celebration, these two women chose to use "my Lady" and "Mother" as feminine images of the Divine.)

> Alexandria: Donna, before I join my life with yours, I wish to acknowledge the promises I have made in brokenness: I made these promises with the best of intentions. I did not break them lightly, and I know the pain that resulted as those dreams dissolved. I regret the pain I have caused others and I mourn the brokenness that did not permit healthy choices. But my Lady is a forgiving and a demanding teacher, and She has called me to make myself in Her image. After much work, much prayer, and much thought, I am whole of heart and ready to relinquish ancient promises to make room for the heartfelt commitment I have for you.
>
> Donna: Alexandria, before I join my life with yours . . . (repeats)
>
> People: I have made promises in my brokenness which had little chance for success. I too have caused pain when I could not be steadfast in relationship or work. Today I confess my sorrow for

dreams that have died and for those I have wounded. Let this be the day that I embrace the fullness of who I am. Let this be the day that I accept forgiveness that I might move on in my life. Let us do this on this occasion where love has triumphed over doubt and wholeness is celebrated by all.

All: Sweet Mother, ever merciful, we give thanks for Your love for Your people. Call our names that we might hear You over our brokenness. Shout Your joy that we might be re-membered from our confusion. Remind us of the fullness of Your image that we might grow into wholeness. Let today be the day. Let Your joy be ours. Let our promises of steadfastness and surety be Your delight in the world.

Celebrant: My Sisters and Brothers, we are always forgiven. May we make our lives a reflection of our dreams. Blessed be.

Wonderful Memories

What of ceremonies where the couple has been involved in other long and happy relationships? I worked with a widow and widower, Rosemary and Herbert, who had each been married previously for over thirty years. Both had suffered terribly as their spouses slowly died from cancer. They were not interested in denying earlier loves; rather, they were interested in applying what they had learned to this new relationship. They were also awestruck, because it had never occurred to them that, after a long, sad period, there would be new love to give meaning to their lives. They knew how precious life was and didn't intend to waste a minute of it.

They wanted to share what they knew with their communities. Some of their children, parents, and friends were having a hard time adjusting to sensible old Herb transformed by joy and choosing a new relationship!

We worked carefully to craft a wedding ceremony in which they acknowledged all the love that they had known in their lives. The two of them chose to speak candidly about their former loves rather than ignore them altogether, or have a stranger to their community (me) speak euphemistically about their earlier lives. When we finished the ceremony, they felt both seen and united, because they made promises to one another that were grounded in their real abilities to keep promises; their communities felt comforted that earlier lives had not been discarded for this new life and love. It was a very moving and powerful ceremony.

Children from Former Relationships

If there are children from earlier relationships, it is important to acknowledge those children and the primacy of the parent-child relationship. In too many second marriages, a never-married spouse or a spouse with no children would like to act as if the children don't exist. This is completely unfair to either the parent or the children. Children are a great and sacred gift — and unlike most of us, are unafraid of expressing their feelings. They will make their presence known and demand a response. The following is an excerpt from Susanne and Michael's ceremony; they married after being together for almost ten years — throughout the school years of Michael's children, Alisa and Jacob.

78

Susanne and Michael, this marriage that you have made between you is, in the final analysis, a partnership that you make with one another. But your life together has always included Michael's children. Do you promise today that the steadfast love you have shared with these two will always be theirs?

We do.

And, Alisa and Jacob, you have welcomed Susanne and her relationship with your dad into your life as you have grown to adulthood. Today they have asked you to witness and support them as they make their promises to one another. Do you promise today that the steadfast love you have shared with these two will always be theirs?

We do.

In the second excerpt, both Wayne and Kate had children. Wayne's two daughters were teenagers. Kate's daughter was still a very little girl. Kate and Wayne would play different roles in each other's children's lives, but both roles would be important. Wayne's daughters did not yet know Kate or Julia well, so they needed to be asked what their intentions would be toward this marriage and the new family that would be created when Wayne moved in with Kate and Julia:

Wayne and Kate, your marriage is ultimately a relationship between the two of you. But it is important to acknowledge that you each come to this marriage with very important relationships that were begun and established before you embarked upon this phase of your relationship. In a very large way those relationships determine who you are in your lives as adults. Any promises you make to one another must recognize the importance and the sweetness of your vocations as parents.

Kate and Wayne, your relationship has always included his two daughters. Wayne has a primary bond and responsibility to Erika and Gretchen. Are you willing to support him in his love and care for his daughters? Are you willing to open your heart and your family to these two young women so that you might find your places in each other's lives?

I am.

Wayne, your relationship has always included Kate's daughter. Kate has a primary bond and responsibility to Julia. Are you willing to support her in her love and care for her daughter? Are you willing to open your heart and your family to this little one so that you might find your places in each other's lives?

I am.

Gretchen and Erika, your father is entering into matrimony with Kate and making space in his life for her daughter Julia. Are you willing to support him in these new and important relationships? And are you willing to open your hearts and family to these two so that you might find your places in each other's lives?

We are.

Commitment Ceremonies for Lesbians and Gay Men

At this time there is a huge debate about who can legally marry. Gays and lesbians find themselves on both sides of the debate. On the one hand they want all the rights and responsibilities of any other couple. On the other hand, many question the worth of an institution that hasn't seemed very effective for straight people in the last twenty-five years, with less than fifty percent of the couples enjoying long-term relationships.

I believe that all couples willing to do the work for healthy, loving and enduring relationship should be allowed to marry. And because I believe that the law does not supercede the wisdom of the heart, I can provide a meaningful ceremony for those who are unwelcome in religious or legal territory.

As states and courts grapple with this dilemma and it remains unresolved, there are certain things you can do to protect yourselves, if you are one of the unrecognized couples.

Publicly proclaim your relationship. "This is who we are and this is how we love each other." Be clear about how this loving relationship changes your life, so everyone can comprehend the enormity and sacredness of the connection. Inviting people uncomfortable with homosexual union to your ceremony may not cause a life-long transformation in them, but I have never seen a ceremony fail to cause at least a momentary epiphany when the community understands that for this moment they are standing in the face of a love whose name must be spoken.

Do the legal work needed to protect yourselves. While most people are good-willed and good-hearted, tragedy and crisis often subvert good judgment. It is important to be legally protected as each other's partners. You need to clarify your relationship in terms of legal and medical issues: housing, insurance, power of attorney. Any local (friendly) attorney can help you with this.

If you cannot receive a marriage license from the state, ask your communities to sign your marriage vows. This calls on two traditions: the first is the Jewish notion of the Ketubah, or the illuminated wedding vows, which are signed. The second is a tradition from the Society of Friends. There is no priestly figure in this tradition (because *all* are priestly figures), so the entire community witnesses the marriage vows by signing them.

After the community signs such documents, these beautifully calligraphed and painted vows are hung in the couple's house as a reminder of their community's support. Many straight couples who have seen these also wish to seek the same kind of support from their communities. They understand that the community support is worth every bit as much as the legal documents.

> Ritual moves us from one place to another. At the end of this ceremony Sharon and Janice will be married in every way but in the eyes of the law. As you know, as lesbians they may not marry legally, nor are they welcome to proclaim their love for one another in most of the churches of this world.
>
> But we who are here today believe that they have every incentive and every right to claim their love — and their love is one that dares to speak its name out loud.
>
> So they have taken two steps to ensure that their relationship will be lifted up and seen as con-

secrated and binding. First, they have made a legal contract with one another to be each other's life partners, responsible to one another and for one another. Secondly, they are asking you to sign their wedding vows and reinforce the verbal promise you have just made.

Their foray into matrimony is as bold and as tentative as any other newlyweds', but the demands on them will be much greater as they negotiate the difficulties of finding jobs and creating a family in a world that by and large neither understands nor supports their partnership. They desire tangible evidence of your support and a daily reminder that they may call upon you in times of need and in times of celebration. The document will be on a table at the reception. We ask those of you who are willing to sign the document during the reception as a sign of your support for their marriage.

Handfasting

Some couples do not wish to mrry legally. There may be money issues or other complications that make legal marriage unattractive, yet the couple wishes to solemnize their vows either alone or before their community. In Wiccan and Pagan traditions and in certain women's traditions, there is a ritual known as "handfasting." For rituals that are true to those traditions, you should seek information from Wiccan or Pagan authors, or on the ever-present, ever-helpful Internet. I have no trouble as a celebrant performing these ceremonies, as long as they are not unethical. I would not handfast two people already married to someone else, for example, and I would not handfast couples not old enough to marry legally.

My concern with relationship is the emotional, spiritual, physical and financial commitment to one another. If a couple is not marrying yet, for what seem like well thought-out reasons, then I am happy to help them pledge themselves to one another or celebrate a promise that they have been living in faith. Traditional handfastings were for a year and a day. I'm less eager to do that unless I'm in a long-term pastoral relationship with a couple who signs up to renew their vows on a yearly basis.

Below is the text for a handfasting ceremony which introduces the vows a couple offers one another. The example given is crafted for a lesbian ceremony. I have used this ceremony in just about every conceivable situation, as the mutuality and free will of it are attractive not only to people who will have only their word, their witnesses and their handclasp to bind them together.

> In Europe, until the mid-1700s, few unions were sanctified in a church or synagogue. Rather, they were celebrated by a simple handfasting ceremony in which the two partners joined hands over the village anvil, in the fields or in a grove of trees. There is evidence that some form of this ceremony was performed, at different times and places in European history, for women who wished to form a family. Today we build upon the strength of that evidence and participate in the shaping of history. The couple linked hands to form an infinity circle, symbolizing the entirety of the universe as represented in their relationship — like flowing into

unlike and, from there, returning. Two people, in a simple act of will, joined hands before their community and became family. In this ancient ceremony is found a mutuality we might not expect, but one which we do well to celebrate today. Standing as equals, they offered their hands to one another and made a commitment to be partners for the rest of their lives — partners in work, in play, in sorrow, in laughter and in love.

Please now join your hands, first right to right, and then left to left. As you stand so joined, pause for a moment to reflect both on your individual gifts and talents as well as your loving union.

Renewal of Vows

Years ago I read an essay about marriage which pointed out that originally couples had had their own separate jobs (women worked in the house and men, in the fields; women were in the garden, men went hunting). Marriage was a convenient and necessary financial and social contract between the couples. Now we expect, of ourselves and of our partners, that we will be everything to each other. The author suggested this was difficult, if not impossible! Later she talked about the fact that marriage agreements change constantly as the jobs and roles of a couple change.

In the face of this thought, it makes sense to rededicate ourselves to our marriages and to celebrate the time we have spent together. It is important in these moments to remember what our first dreams were with one another, and what the realities are now and what our next dreams are. I would use very much the same format as for first weddings — but I would do a lot more of the writing myself if it were mine.

You might want a celebrant or priest to bless the vows, but you might just want to make your own vows to one another (or remake your original vows) in front of your community.

It's a beautiful tradition to say that a loving relationship is important enough to be celebrated. It's hard to sustain a loving relationship — so if you're still managing after ten, twenty or thirty years, let the world know! Acknowledge what has been difficult and revel in what has given meaning and joy to your life together.

Chapter 6
Your Family Is Always
Your Family

Disapproving Parents

In a perfect world, our families are on board for all the most important events in our lives: enthusiastic and supportive, they stand with us as we step forward into our futures. But not everyone receives that kind of support from their families. I believe that most families *want* to give us that kind of support. Some don't know how; some find the circumstances of our lives too far outside their own understanding of the world. If your family is unable to give you their support, this will be one of the hardest things you will deal with as you prepare for your wedding and your life with your partner.

You and your partner must be clear with yourselves and with each other about how you will deal with the difficulties that arise. There are problem periods that will occur as you plan your wedding, in the week or so before your ceremony, the day of your wedding, and as your marriage goes on. The more carefully you look at the problems and work out solutions beforehand, the less painful and disruptive those moments will be. You deserve a wonderful wedding, and planning around the problems will help ensure that you have one. *The clearer you are about what you want, the better able your family is to make a decision about how they can participate in your wedding.*

One of the best things you can do for yourself is to seek counseling. A good counselor can help you work on both short- and long-term ways of coping with family issues. In the short term, your celebrant can be helpful as you plan the ceremony in finding ways that invite and/or acknowledge your families' biases while establishing a framework that represents you honestly and demands acknowledgment of your special relationship.

Randy's parents were unable to accept that their 30-year-old son had lived with his fiancee before they married. They refused to recognize his relationship with "that woman," refused to come to the wedding and would not permit his brothers and sisters to come either. We did as much as we could to help Randy and Marci get clear about how they felt about his parents' inability to celebrate them and their relationship.

The couple asked Randy's grandfather to represent the family, and that helped enormously. They acknowledged that there were many family members not in attendance who were sorely missed. And then they went on with the happiness in their lives.

It was quite a bit later that everything worked out — but what was important was that the couple knew what they wanted, what it felt like not getting it, and were prepared to look for it further down the road — on their own terms. She's now carrying their first baby and the grandparents are counting the days! That doesn't remove the hurt, but at least their expectations are now those of adults and not children whose parents are hurting them. It's a horrible way to grow up in a hurry, but both Randy and Marci were aware that their happiness was the most important thing in their life — and so they did the work.

There will always be problems with families. They're complicated: that's their nature. With planning and counseling, you can make the best of a situation, and often that enables the situation to change. But it pays to do your homework, figure out what could go wrong and plan around the worst-case scenario. Then, since what you get is almost always better than what you fear, you're prepared!

Unfriendly Family Breakups

Probably the most complicated thing I deal with as a celebrant is helping my couples when there are family issues to sort out. This manifests most commonly in situations with divorced parents. Many divorced parents made the decision long ago to be adult about their former relationship and deal with each other and the children in a way that encourages and supports the children's lives. There are many wonderful stories that I could tell here, but what concerns me are the parents who are unable to do this for their children.

It is unacceptable that parents — or any family member — use their children's important moments as opportunities to act out. While I can make every effort to free my couples from responsibility for managing their parents' relationship on their special day, it is incumbent upon the parents to work this out beforehand.

Notes for Parents

Whether parents are divorced or still happily married, there is work for couples whose children are marrying to do. Remember why you married. If you're divorced, you no doubt have a catalogue about why you're divorced (most of it having to do with your ex's faults), but there are reasons why you married in the first place. I believe that most marriages are made for good reasons, however misguided or misunderstood. When we make major life decisions, we use the best abilities we have at the time to make them. It may be, at sometime after your marriage, you realize there was information you should have had or judgments you might have made differently. At that time, however, you were thinking as clearly as you knew how, and with all the hope and optimism that everyone brings to a marriage.

On this day, and on every other important social occasion in your child's life, it's important to remember this. It's important to say to yourself, perhaps to your spouse, and certainly to your child: "I'm so glad that my relationship produced such a wonderful child. I'm proud of us all."

To aid this process, I've designed a worksheet for the parents. (You'll find it in the appendix on page 109.) You don't need to be divorced or separated to reflect on your relationship — these are good things to think about in any marriage. If you really want this to work, for your child and as an aid for putting history in perspective, it's helpful not to use this as simply an opportunity to catalogue your partner's (or former partner's) faults.

There is no reason your child's wedding shouldn't be an amazing personal triumph for you as well as for your child! There are important lessons for you here and it's an incomparable gift to your child. A wedding is truly something to celebrate — so enjoy.

Find some family or personal friends who will support you throughout the day. Finding someone to run interference is not cowardly; it's the responsible thing to do, for yourself and for your child. If there are bad feelings, they must be put aside for the good of your child. This will not be the first — or even the last — time you make compromises for the good of your child. For better or worse, this is what you signed on for when you chose to have a child with another person. Your lives are forever joined through this bond.

Parents Unhappy with Your Sexual Orientation

For the most part, the parents at my gay unions have been supportive and enthusiastic about their children's relationships. One particularly moving instance involved a mother who was quite ill. She pushed her daughter, Jackie, and her partner, Janna, to get clear about their commitment to one another, and if it felt appropriate to Janna and Jackie, to have a ceremony in which the mom could take an active role before she became too ill. It was an amazing ceremony, and the families gave those two women the support that everyone would like to have from those they love.

Unfortunately, there are still people who have difficulty seeing gay relationships as "normal." Often, parents' love for their children will enable them to look past their prejudices about who you are and how you live. *A ceremony that clearly proclaims your love for one another, and allows families and friends to grasp the sheer normalcy of your living as loving partners, is all that is needed and can usually soften the most hardened hearts.* In the tenderness of that moment, even family members who swore they came to this ceremony only on sufferance are able to speak up and offer you their support for the relationship. In most situations, there is work to be done beforehand. Your decision to spend the rest of your life with another person is a momentous one. You deserve all the support available as you enter into a committed life together.

Be clear with yourself and with your families if you want them to be at your wedding. Even if you think that they won't be able to manage being there, you must know and say what you want. If you don't ask for what you want, there is very little chance that you will get it. If you do ask directly, you are far more likely to get an honest and respectful answer.

Couples receive both "yes" and "no" to their requests to family members. Linda asked her mother to come, but she didn't want her father present because he had been so outspoken in his opinion about her life and her choices. Her mother made the decision not to attend without him. While the daughter (and probably her mother) was heartbroken, at least she managed the situation in such a way as to not have her pain overwhelm the wedding day. She spoke to her family months before the ceremony, and thus was able to have some time to cope with her feelings before the day of the ritual. Family friends from her childhood made the decision to come from quite far away once they heard that her parents would not be there. While she missed her parents, she was able to celebrate her wedding day and not have it overshadowed by her disappointment. Planning made all the difference for her.

Janice's parents initially felt unable to attend because they had religious and moral difficulties with their daughter's life. Her first thought was that all she needed from her parents was an acknowledgment that, whether or not they agreed with who she was, this moment and this action were among the most important of her life. She called her parents. They all talked, they all shouted, and they all cried. At the end of the conversation, her parents could and did acknowledge the importance of her union. When Janice hung up the phone, her parents still weren't coming, but she felt she had accomplished what she set out to do. She soon discovered, to her surprise, that acknowledgment wasn't enough. She wanted her parents to be there, whether or not they "approved." She called them back and said exactly that. Once they understood just how important it was to her that they attend, they agreed. By the time the weekend was over and we were in the midst of the ceremony where the family was asked to welcome Sharon into the family, Janice's parents were proud and happy to do so. It was an amazing moment for everyone: parents, daughter, brother, partner, Celebrant. I cried throughout the whole ceremony.

Asking for what you want is important. You might wind up with exactly what you asked for. Even if you can't have what you want, know what you are going to get in a given situation. Don't spend the time leading up to your wedding in wild mood swings about someone's approval. Ask your questions, get your answers and deal with the results. Preparation makes your life different and that can make all the difference in your ability to enjoy your wedding.

Parents Unhappy You are Marrying Outside Your Clan

Remember Romeo and Juliet? People want to be married, and they long for their parents' support. Acknowledging your differences and your individuality during the ceremony can go a long way toward healing your family's fears. You don't need to acknowledge or dwell on their prejudices. You can tell them that you hear them, but that your happiness lies in your partner's arms.

For many of us, problems that parents have with intermarriage seem very outmoded. For people who lived through the worst of segregation and the civil rights movement, for immigrants whose families suffered terribly under the Holocaust, for those who endured an enormous amount to come to this country — it can be very difficult to let go of old animosities and prejudices. We need to be understanding about that.

Most parents want their children's happiness more than anything, and they will do everything they can to bless your marriage. It is worth your while to help them see how truly happy you are with this person. However, if they cannot accept your marriage to your partner, you need to decide how you will cope with this at your wedding ceremony and throughout the rest of your lives together. Dealing with this issue up front, probably with the help of an excellent counselor, can improve your marriage's chances for success.

Family Dynamics and Issues

I don't believe the old saw that "anything that can go wrong, will." However, if there are situations that might arise to cause discomfort, it's best to know what they could be. Are there people who don't get along? Are there physical limitations that need to be thought through and provided for?

John and Robert wanted to be married outside at a place that wasn't wheelchair accessible, and one of the dads was in a wheelchair. The men were asked beforehand to help carry the wheelchair out to the field. It was easily handled — it just needed to be planned. The planning that was done meant that the dad felt cared for and the friends felt useful. The couple didn't need to fret about it on the wedding day, because the problem was solved ahead of time.

My experience at most weddings is that people are on their best behavior. But there are occasions where my experience has been disproved. Planning can minimize the problems. Friends and family members are always glad to help you deal with whatever might happen, but they do a much better job if they are aware of possible problems.

Chapter 7
Where to Find Your Celebrant

Wedding magazines and books seem to believe that most people are still being married in religious settings and therefore have access to religious leaders. While many couples are being married in churches and synagogues, many are not. This is particularly true in the Bay Area where I live. In part this is because there are so many urban professionals here who no longer live in their community of birth or their community of faith; in part this is because there are so many mixed marriages here in this metropolitan area.

It's not always easy to find someone who will pay careful attention to what you want and who also has the ability to conduct your ceremony in a meaningful way. While booking your place is important, the person who will help bring meaning to your day is very important to find. Determine what you want in a ceremony and find the person most likely to give it to you.

If you've decided upon something other than a church or courthouse wedding, it can be tricky to find someone to officiate your wedding. Look in newspapers, especially in their special bridal sections. Check out the alternative newspapers. Talk to the people at the location you've chosen; they often keep good records of celebrants and vendors they like. Talk to your caterer or photographer. Wedding magazines sometimes have local listings. A Bay Area publishing company, Hopscotch Press, publishes a book called *Here Comes the Guide*, which provides useful information about vendors. They've started to publish guides to other regions — and other groups are probably doing the same. Wedding consultants are excellent sources. You might need to be a little creative in your looking. Ask your friends for recommendations. There is an amazing amount of information on the web now, so browse away.

Do You Want a Religious or Secular Ceremony?

This is the most important decision and will determine where you look for someone to marry you. If you're an interfaith couple, or you've been living together, these things may present obstacles for certain clergy members. But if you're clear about what you want, you can usually get most of your needs met.

Your States' Laws About Celebrants

In California anyone over 18 can get a license for a day to perform a ceremony. This has its drawbacks as well as its advantages. On the plus side, if your friend does perform your wedding, your celebrant will know you well. (Make sure you pick someone who will ensure everyone will hear the ceremony. Being audible is really important.) If you're lucky, they will know something about ritual and relationship and have some idea what they want to say. Wedding ceremonies need form and require certain actions. It's wise to provide good resources (like this book!) for whomever you choose.

California licenses people to perform wedding

ceremonies who are not associated with religious groups; judges are licensed to marry you, and licensed and ordained ministers and rabbis are authorized by their religious tradition to perform wedding ceremonies. In some states justices of the peace and notaries public can preside at your wedding. Your local county courthouse will be able to tell you. Many counties now have web sites that list all these details and also tell you how to get a wedding license.

Great Weddings You've Been To

Whose weddings do you remember? What were the things that made it great? Did the celebrant know the couple? Were the readings interesting? Was the celebrant engaging? What about really boring or uncomfortable weddings? What made them not work for you? Review all this together before you meet your candidates.

Services Vary

What kind of training have people had? This is not to say that only seminary-trained clergy will do good work, or that seminary training is a guarantee of meaningful ritual, but being knowledgeable about the customs of marriage rituals and rituals themselves can be an important clue in choosing a person to perform your ceremony.

How much of their work is performing weddings and other rituals? Is it a part of their job that they take seriously, or simply something they backed into doing as a sideline? How long have they been doing this? How many weddings have they performed?

You have a right to know all these things. You don't need to meet with everyone to find out: use the telephone as a screening process. Meet three or four people, unless you find someone who is simply perfect right away.

Interview the Candidates

Make a list of what matters to you and then listen very closely while the celebrant explains what she or he does. If your questions don't come up, ask them. If you remember something later that will help in your decision-making, call the person back. This is a really important decision. Make it early enough to get some choice.

Will this person write especially for you? Will he or she be willing to read what you want said? What is his or her philosophy about marriage and ritual? You have a right to know how they believe the ceremony can impact your life. If you don't click with someone, despite their vast store of knowledge, this is not your celebrant for this important day. If their answers don't fit with your desires, however nice this person may be, they may not be right to perform your ceremony.

Fees: Expect to Pay for What You Want

I know, I know, weddings are expensive. But the words that join you together need to be able to last a lifetime. Goodness knows, we don't want that *wedding cake* on our hips for a lifetime — and wedding cakes cost a great deal of money. A wedding ceremony that is crafted especially for you will cost from a few hundred to a few thousand dollars, depending upon the services the celebrant provides.

If you need the celebrant at the rehearsal the night before the ceremony, and the ceremony is out of town, you'll need to find a room for the celebrant. If they have to travel to get to your event, most celebrants will charge you for travel time. In the Bay Area, it can take as much as two hours to get 40-50 miles, and that's simply lost time for your celebrant. (And of course, if someone is flying, you'll be expected to pick up the airfare.)

A good celebrant is worth the cost. The words that reflect and structure your loving relationship and commitment are worth at least as much as the cake or the flowers.

Chapter 8
Benediction

The process of getting married can be fraught with details and crises. Planning your wedding ceremony can be a wonderful anchor in the midst of the chaos. It should draw you closer together and remind you how much you love one another — and why! A lovely by-product is that it gives you a way to stay centered and have a good time as you prepare for something that can be far more daunting than marriage: a wedding! I offer you this book as a way to deepen your commitment to one another and to think seriously about the ways you wish to shape your life, even as you prepare to say "I love you today, and I will love you for as long as I live."

Use this book!

Enjoy it!

Get ready to enjoy the rest of your life spent in each other's company!

Lovers, live joyously into this solemn endeavor and live happily in love and respect, now and forever.

Blessed be!

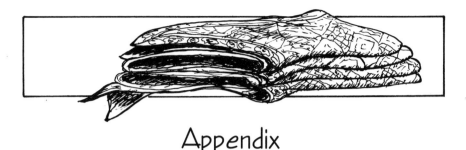

Appendix

Essential Elements of a Wedding Ceremony

Introduction / Invitation: Why we are here today, what you are affirming, and before whom (your families, your communities, Spirit).

Invocation: Includes a consecration of the space, the occasion, and the gathered community. If you wish to have a religious ceremony, acknowledge Spirit here.

Joining the Families: Acknowledges that both families are being enriched by the couple's joining.

Statement of Intent: Explains why you wish to marry and why it's appropriate to make this change now. It is an opportunity to explain how your commitment will impact your life and that of your community and what you celebrate in your life together.

Statement of Support: Allows the gathered community to offer their verbal support of your relationship. As your community they assume the responsibility to support you and your relationship in times of stress as well as in times of joy.

Images of Relationship: A perfect place for songs, poems, or statements from your friends and family.

Charge to the Couple: Celebrant's understanding of marriage, both within the context of loving relationships through time and of your personal relationship.

Vows: Affirms your choice to marry and make your promises to each other. You may wish to use traditional words or find new words to celebrate your love.

Exchange of Rings: Explains the meaning of the exchange of rings through time and what it means today to wear each other's rings.

Proclamation and Blessing: Acknowledges the difference in your lives because of the promises you have made. Provides a blessing for the future.

Benediction: Dismisses the gathering and reminds them of their promise to support your loving relationship.

Worksheet for Statement of Intent

1. Tell how you and your partner met.

2. Tell your relationship story (include why you're marrying now).

3. What are the qualities your partner possesses that cause you to love her/him?

4. What are the qualities your partner possesses that challenge you to grow?

5. When you are with your partner, in what ways do you feel most truly yourself?

6. When you are with your partner, do you feel safe to venture beyond the ways you have always done things? In what ways?

7. Why do you think that you could make this relationship last a lifetime? Why is an enduring marriage of value?

8. What are the things that would cause this marriage to end?

9. On your wedding day, what do you wish to say to your partner?

10. As you get married, what do you wish your community to know about your relationship and your love for your partner?

11. Have you decided what to do about money, church/ God, children? Whose job would you move for? Would you take in your own parents? Would you take in your partner's parents? Do you know if you and your partner are in agreement about these issues?

12. Write your Statement of Intent.

Worksheet for Your Vows

What does it mean in this day and age to make an oath? It is not something frequently done. Wedding vows may be the only oaths you swear during your adult life. In an oath, each word, each phrase, should be one you can envision honoring. Not all that long ago, a person's word was their bond. These days, it's easy to establish legal qualifications and boundaries about the sharing of lives — but a marriage vow, solemnized before a community, and if you will, before the Divine, is a covenant of hearts and lives. You have placed your integrity on the line by making a promise. It is not something to be done lightly.

It's rather naive to believe that abandoning a vow makes it less binding or influential in your life. Whether or not you remain in day-to-day relationship with a person, the vows you make to your partner will change and shape you for the rest of your life. On this important day, make the right vows for the right reasons. Know, even if you leave the relationship, those vows have an existence all their own. If you wish to make new vows, you must unmake these — and acknowledge their power. If you have children together in a marriage, you must search out and hold as holy those things that caused you to bring them into this world — because the children are sacred. To do less is to disrepect your offspring and the very real and important choices you made with all the wisdom you could bring to bear on that moment in your life.

With the sacredness and solemnity of this effort in mind, use the lists below to begin to imagine the promises you can make.

Who you are to me: companion, confidant, friend, lover, partner, spouse (wife, husband)

What will I do? believe, cherish, honor, listen, love, nurture, promise, respect, share, support, trust

What will I offer? acceptance, commitment, compromise, doubts, faith, fears, fidelity, friendships, family, gentleness, growth, honesty, joy, laughter, monogamy, passion, presence, priority, reflection, resources, sacrifice, self-respect, sorrow, spirituality, truth, uncertainties

When will I offer it? as we grow and change, as we grow old, forever and ever, in sickness and health, in times of conflict, in private times and public, until death do us part, when it is easy and hard, when we are afraid, when we are confused, when we have erred

Worksheet for Parents

This worksheet was designed to help divorced parents gain perspective about their marriage to their child's other parent before the wedding. There are good questions here for *all* parents to review before important events in your children's lives. You made the best choices you could when you married this person. This is an opportunity to remember those reasons.

1. Why did we get together and choose to marry? What attracted me to my partner?

2. Remember three times in the past which were fun and embodied the good times of your relationship.

3. If you are no longer married, what is it in you that changed your ability or desire to remain in relationship? Understanding that your partner was always fully the person you married and that you just were unable to see a full picture, what made you think that it was time to move on?

4. Have you made peace with yourself for your former relationship? With your former spouse? Are you willing or able to do this for this event? Are you aware of ways your feelings about your former relationship interrupt your present life and relationships?

5. If you're still married: what do you now know about yourself and your partner that makes the maintenance work you have done to sustain your marriage an effort well worth making? Are there things to be addressed before the

wedding that will make the wedding more poignant for you and your relationship?

6. Are you willing to do what is necessary so your child will have a wonderful day? Do you understand that this is your problem, not your child's, to solve?

7. What is uncomfortable for you? If you are unhappy about someone's presence, or your own ability to cope, how will you take responsibility for being comfortable to make things easier for your child? What are your fears? Unrealistic expectations? If you felt as if you had no control in this relationship — how can you change that balance now? (Short-term counseling, separately or together, the presence of a stable and steady good friend, other children's help in keeping the two of you separate, clarity about the way this person always annoyed you and ways to ignore it.)